Hazel Court
HORROR QUEEN

An Autobiography

by Hazel Court

First published in 2008 by
Tomahawk Press
PO Box 1236
Sheffield S11 7XU
England
www.tomahawkpress.com

ISBN-10: 0-9531926-8-7
ISBN-13: 978-0-9531926-8-7

Edited by Bruce Sachs

Proof-read by Kenneth Bishton – kenbishton@onetel.com

Designed by Tree Frog Communication 01245 445377

Printed in the EU by Gutenberg Press Limited

Picture Credits
Many pictures in this book are owned and supplied by the author, © Hazel Court Taylor. In other cases copyright is retained by the original owners. If we have inadvertently published a photograph without credit, please contact the publishers so that the omission can be corrected in the next printing. Thanks to David Del Valle for providing some great photos of Hazel.

Front cover photo from the writer's private collection and used with the permission of Roger Corman.

A catalogue record for this book is available from the British Library.

Who could ask for more? You might even get Hazel Court wandering around in a lacy low-cut nightgown, if you were lucky.

Stephen King – On Writing

Hodder and Stoughton 2000

Hazel in Stockholm – modelling Horracks Cotton

DEDICATION

This book is dedicated to my very special children – my two different Celts:
My Irish Sally Walsh -and- My Scottish Jonathan Taylor
Without your love and caring, I would have been long gone after my beloved Don died.

And
My beloved husband Don Taylor

K
K

Q
Q

From Vincent…

Is there anything more delightful than to know someone who is completely consistent? In this complex world, it's a rarity and a joy!

Hazel Court is just such a human being. She paints as she is, as she talks, as she lives. She lives and works in the reality of romance, in the now of nostalgia.

What she sees and records is her vision uncluttered by a world of art ego gone mad. She lets the life around her live its own life, which is very personally hers too. Her pictures present her world of desires and ones you feel will all be fulfilled in her pictures and herself.

Vincent Price
(on an exhibition of Hazel Court paintings)

“Hazel Court is one of the most beautiful and talented actresses that I have ever had the pleasure of directing. We made three pictures together: The Premature Burial, The Raven and The Masque of Red Death. With more than sixty major screen roles to her credit, she managed to truly find herself within each character that she took on – a feat accomplished by only the most talented and focused of professional actors. Her unique approach to each role has endeared her to generations of movie lovers and her grace and presence in these films are legendary in their own right.

In these pages of her marvellous book, Hazel tells her own story in a way that only she could do, allowing the reader to find the real Hazel within. And what a marvellous thing that is! I enjoyed this book very much as will you.

Roger Corman
March 2008

“I always knew that Hazel Court was a great sculptor and artist, but a great writer, no way! Well, Hazel fooled everybody. Hazel Court – Horror Queen is a fabulous autobiography. I feel that I now know everybody from Grandma Blockley to Hazel's first husband, Dermot Walsh; from the director Roger Corman to my great friend, the director Don Taylor. I can even visualise the houses Hazel lived in. Hazel's recollection of the past is amazing. She is a truly great writing talent, as you are about to find out. Enjoy!

Harvey Bernhard
Producer of the Omen series
March 2008

"Hazel Court – Horror Queen" is a book you will enjoy, remember, and tell others they must read. It is filled with wonderful anecdotes of people and places she met and experienced over many years. I first met Hazel when I was casting 'Holiday Camp'. This beautiful young lady walked into the Casting Office at Shepherd's Bush Studio and I knew she would be right for the part of a lonely single mother with a baby. Her performance was original and touching and after this movie she went on to make films of many kinds and eventually becoming the Queen of Horror movies.

This book recounts memories of her early childhood in the British Midlands and the people who would influence her in her life - her mother, father, aunts, etc. and then her voyage into movies all over the world and her eventual marriage to Don Taylor, the famous actor and director with whom she lived happily for over thirty-five years.

It is a remarkable book insofar as she tells how, whenever she was approaching stage or film parts, she used her experience and remembrances of real people and real places to help her create characters...

Her portrayals, time and time again, result in being original whether she is playing someone attractive or horrible. If you know Hazel you love her as I have done for sixty years.

Ken Annakin
Beverly Hills, California
March 2008

Foreword

By Sally Walsh

Palmer – a ten-something year old Ford Bronco, with a paint job that gives him the appearance of a rusted pinto pony – is the pride of my mother's life. With its faded, ripped, worn out, olive-brown cloth interior that challenges this viewer's sense of style, Palmer is one of two cars my mother, The Scream Queen presently owns. Out of the two, Palmer has the singular honour of being inducted into the Hazel Court Auto Hall of Fame. Sadly, Palmer's sibling – a pretty white Ford Sable – is referred to only as "the Sable."

Palmer and the Sable live outside our cabin, high in the Sierra wilderness, on a winding trail that Indians used to walk, surrounded by bears and wolves – yes, they really are there, and we have many photos. At the cabin there are also packs of coyotes, chipmunks, squirrels, birds galore, and of course, Palmer and Sable's loving driver – my mother.

Another inductee into the Hazel Court Auto Hall of Fame was called Woofie. It was while sitting beside my mother in Woofie – a dear, rather drab Austin A40, circa 1955 – that I was first startlingly struck by Mum's incredible beauty. That moment, as clear today as forty-eight years ago, was a revelation.

She was driving, the sunlight streaming into the car, and as I glanced across from the passenger seat, there was that face with its perfect bone structure, its trim, fine-boned nose, a cascade of blazing auburn hair, and translucent skin. I was mesmerised. I couldn't wait for her to say something and become real again, for her to just be Mum.

Soon after this, Mum and I got ourselves into a scrape where her beauty saved the day. One day, on the way to Kensington for lunch, Woofie, Mum and I were charging through St. James's Park toward Buckingham Palace.

"Look, Sally," Mum cried, "the Union Jack [flag] is flying. The Queen is home!"

Suddenly, there was a loud thud as something dropped in front of us. Mother pounced on the brakes and we gasped. A hand appeared on Woofie's bonnet. Then another hand appeared. Then, an entire policeman crawled up in front of us. Clearly furious, he dusted off his shoulders, repositioned his bobby's hat and painfully lumbered toward the driver's window.

Mum whispered, "We are in for it."

Slowly he bent his head down towards her, and yelled, "Do you know what you just did?"

Mum murmured, "I am so sorry."

Above: Hazel in one of her many glamour shots

He bent in closer and squinted quizzically, and then suddenly a huge beaming smile stretched across his face.

We froze.

"Are you Hazel Court?" he asked.

"Yes, I am," Mum replied.

"I am such a fan of yours, Miss Court," he continued.

Pulling out a notebook, he handed it to Mum, who autographed it. "Miss Court," he cooed with delight, "you can knock me down any time."

When I was growing up, it took me awhile to understand just what the show business thing was all about. After all, Hazel Court was Mum to me.

I grew up in the garden county of Kent in a small whitewashed cottage. At that time, a lot of actors raised their families in the country to keep the kids away from the hectic lives they lived in London. Sir John Mills and his family were up the road, the Attenboroughs were not far away, and there were several other celebrity families.

It was quite a sacrifice to live where we lived. Mum and Dad – another physically gorgeous person – faced a long drive to the studios and, if they were doing theatre, a late night ride home after the show.

Mum would come in and tuck me up, her perfume obliterating the ordinary smell of my room. Sometimes she wore magnificent gowns that made her look like an exotic princess, her jewels twinkling in the firelight, as did she. Then Dad – Dermot Walsh – came in for the final tuck-up, with sweet lovely talk about Teddy and me. His voice, a tool of his trade, was to me one of the most wonderful I have ever heard.

The qualities that made Mum and Dad great performers were present in my everyday life; yes, they were magical people.

My mother's body parts were of great interest to everyone, including me. Dad said she had "racehorse legs." I regularly inspected mine. What kind was I going to have? I wondered, considering that an aunt of mine had lollipop legs. "The Hazel Courts" apparently referred to my mum's boobs which everyone seemed very interested in. During the late forties and fifties, she was in every magazine. Her fun-loving sense of humour and light breezy personality endeared her to everyone.

Mum's book reveals that she is truly a Renaissance woman – a performer, traveller, painter, sculptor, writer, photographer and naturalist. Fiercely individual, she explores life on her own terms.

Her great beauty has withstood the years, and people still stop her and remark about that something in her face.

Sally M.J. Walsh
Brentwood, California 2008

ACKNOWLEDGMENTS

I want to thank all the people of Tahoe who made me welcome to the mountains and a new and very different life: Tom Draves, Linda and Tim Granger, the Maloof family, Peter and Joan Graves, Ryrie, the Olsen family, Bob and Bobbie Dalton, Robert and Teresa Ferragamo, and Mr. and Mrs. Andy Vertheim, who sold me the little house which has become known as "Hansel and Gretel's Cottage."

Thank you to all who read my story. It is important to remember one's family and pass them on to history and eternity. This book has been a tremendous experience in my life – learning, remembering, and becoming wiser and wiser. Life is to be lived, loved, and cried over.

To all my friends from teenage years and up (most of you are still alive, although we are creaking a bit) – your friendship has meant a great deal to my life. Thank you. We did have a rollicking good time.

To the wonderful fans I have enjoyed throughout my career – I hope you all enjoy my book. The older ones of you now have children, and when I go for signings, you bring them to meet me. We have a special relationship. Horror film fans are very different and extraordinary people. You are very loyal. Grateful thanks.

To Vivien Cooper, developmental editor, whose sensitive touch to my writing helped me finalise the manuscript for publication – you are the best, the very, very best. Many, many thanks.

To Barbara Cherish – your friendship, encouragement, and continued appreciation of my book kept me going.

My very special thank you to Bruce Sachs, my publisher, whose idea it was for me to write this book. Life pushed me around a bit between the beginning and the finish of my story. Bruce, you were incredibly patient and let me just roll on throughout. The Sachs family is a wonderful family, including Harpur, your marvellous, funny, and beautiful spaniel dog. Through the years I have felt very welcome and part of your family.

Far left: Aunt Annie.

Left: Mary Blockley – Hazel's grandmother.

AUNT ANNIE – THE LADY OF THE WILDFLOWERS

This is how I will always remember her – our beautiful lady leaning on the railing with a certain heaviness, looking every bit like a Monet painting. As the boat made its way across the English Channel, my Grandma Blockley was leaving England for the first time in her life. There she was, dressed all in black but for the white lace at her throat, her golden red hair tucked under a velvet toque. She was travelling from a village in Shropshire, one of the most sparsely populated counties in England.

Grandma Blockley was hurrying to the bedside of her daughter, Annie. Aunt Annie, as our family called her, was seriously ill. She was the governess to Louis, who was the son of Monsieur and Madame le Breton, and she lived with them at a wonderful 16th century chateau called the Château de la Folletière (XVI Siècle) at Neuilly near Paris.

Aunt Annie was the victim of a strange and serious illness that had turned her skin blue. It was a cruel and mysterious fate that the doctors surmised might have been caused by poisoning. Walking in the countryside, gathering armfuls of wildflowers was one of her favourite pastimes. As she bent to dip into the freshwater springs the small silver cup she carried attached to her belt, and raise it to her lips to drink, did she, her doctors wondered, perhaps also swallow a poisonous baby adder? Naturally, over the years, our family would juggle various theories about the actual cause of her deathly illness.

By the time Grandma Blockley reached her bedside, her daughter's life was already ebbing away. My mother Madge, Aunt Annie's sister, had once described Annie to me as the most beautiful girl she had ever seen. Before her illness, she had flowing chestnut coloured hair and a striking and lovely face. Now her eyes of deep green were losing their shine, and her once radiant complexion was turned a sickly ashen blue.

Grandma found Annie laying on her deathbed amid a sea of delicate pink and white May blossoms she had placed there before falling ill. This flower was considered terribly unlucky by the English, but Annie, ever a romantic, would hear none of it. Grandma held her beloved daughter close to her heart, cherishing what she understood would be their last moments together.

Taking from around her neck a thin gold chain with a circle of gold carrying the inscription, "Louis 23 October, 1909," Annie pressed it into her mother's hand. Then, with the whisper of an angel, Annie implored her mother, "Give this to Madge. Tell her to look after George. And to love him."

George and Annie were engaged at the time, but following Aunt Annie's death, Madge would take Annie's admonishment to heart and love George. They would produce a daughter, who would – as I still do to this day – wear Aunt Annie's gold pendant around her neck.

On her return to England, Grandma Blockley suffered a stroke that left a permanent tremor in her left eye. From that moment on, a little tear always resided there. I can see her now – a lovely, proud Welsh woman, holding to her eye a lace handkerchief, trying to calm the twitching.

Grandma Blockley lived in the incredible English countryside, at the foot of the Wrekin, a small mountain in East Shropshire, four miles west of Telford. She was tall and straight as a broom with naturally curly, snow-white hair. She would live to be ninety-two years old, but not long enough to hear the area become known as Cadfael Country, nicknamed for *Cadfael*, the 1994-1996 TV series based upon the murder mystery book series about a fictional detective of the same name, penned by Edith "Ellis Peters" Pargeter.

An athletic woman with a long stride that gave her the appearance of having her feet just slightly off the ground, Grandma Blockley was a great walker and climber, often seen climbing the Wrekin. This was one of her great pleasures, and an important emotional outlet. Her love of climbing and walking was passed down to my mother, and then to me, my daughter Sally and my son Jonathan – mountain goats, all of us.

Above: Aunt Annie's home at the Château de la Folletière (XVI Siècle) at Neuilly near Paris

Alongside her Annie, Grandma had six other children – the boys, Frank and Ernest, and the girls, Mena, Francis, my mother Madge and Alice. Sadly, the loss of her Annie had not been my grandmother's first great loss. Her husband, my Grandfather David, was a handsome Welshman with black hair and eyes of chocolate brown. He had been killed in an accident on the road outside their house, dying right before her eyes. Although the brake was secured, on that icy day, the pony and trap slipped forward on the melting ice as Grandpa David walked toward the front of his horse to pat his nose.

His death was instantaneous – and a devastating blow to Grandma Blockley. She loved her David passionately and carried the shock of his premature death forward with her. She never fully recovered as she trudged on – alone and with very little money – in the raising of their seven little children.

"Every night," my mother told me, "we children had to polish our shoes and put them in front of the fire. And before bed, breakfast was laid at the table for the following morning, with a single penny set beside each plate so we might have milk and biscuits at school. And," she went on, "not one of us was ever excused from the table before each one had finished their breakfast." My mother Madge and Aunt Annie's other siblings all survived the poverty of their youth, and grew to be wonderful human beings with large families of their own. All, of course, except Annie – but then, she was an angel.

I have a postcard of the Château de la Folletière where Aunt Annie lived. Two little crosses on the second floor toward the right turret mark her bedroom and the nursery. As I look to the right on the postcard where I can see a hillside, I experience the strangest feeling. My own Aunt Annie, this fascinating, remarkable lady, walked that very countryside, picking wild flowers and drinking spring water.

G. W. COURT.
The Barnwood House Pro. whose bowling record is commented on in our Notes on Sports and Pastimes.

Above Top: Hazel, her mum, sister Audrey and father G.W. Court

Above: Hazel's father G. W. Court

Right: Hazel's childhood home at Wylde Green – 1927

As I do today while I am writing about her, I often feel Aunt Annie's presence. Thinking about how important she was in my life, I am struck by the fact that in some curious way, my angel, The Lovely Lady of the Wildflowers, gave me permission to be born. She is buried somewhere in Rouen, France. I wish I knew where.

DAD AND THE MAGICAL CRICKET FIELDS

My father, George William Court, was a professional cricketer and quite a star as a fast bowler. In fact, Willington County Cricket Club once presented him with a gold medal bearing the inscription "Mid Durham Senior Cricket League 1924 G.W.C. George William Court." I often wear the medal as a necklace.

My mother Madge was a lovely Welsh lady, very proud of her raven black hair, which she never cut and which flowed down her back in startling contrast to her violet eyes. Every month she would wait for the new moon, and then singe the ends of her hair with a taper to encourage the hair to grow thick. Friday nights brought the ritual washing of her hair with water from the rain barrel, and a strange shampoo called green soft soap. During the war, when all the ladies were sporting smart bobs, surely I thought Mother would cut her hair, but all the way until the end of her life, her hair remained in a coil at the nape of her neck.

Eleven years before my birth, while my parents were living in the North of England at Willington, County Durham – a community whose economy was largely based on coal mining – my sister Audrey, my only sibling, was born. She was as fair as Mother but looked like Father.

I was born a redhead with green eyes, in Birmingham Handsworth, England. When I was ten months old,

Far Left: Hazel's father G. W. Court in 1912

Centre: Hazel's mother at a photography studio in Wylde Green

Below: A news clipping featuring Hazel's father G. W. Court

BRILLIANT BOWLING ACHIEVEMENTS.

Remarkable Feats of G. W. Court of Willington C.C.

Some remarkable performances have been achieved by G. W. Court, hon. secretary and groundsman to the Willington Cricket Club, who takes a well-deserved benefit next Saturday, when Willington entertain Crook Town. Court is one of the best-known cricketers in the Mid-Durham Senior League, and he is exceedingly popular not only because of his great ability as a fast bowler, but also because of his splendid sportsmanship and cheery personality.

G. W. COURT,
the popular Willington cricketer, who takes his benefit next Saturday.

Born at Blackdown, just off the borders of Surrey, Court first came into prominence in local cricket. With the Fernhurst C.C. in 1903 he took 75 wickets for 3.35 runs each, and the next season for Chiddingfold, in Surrey, he had an excellent season. In 1906 we find him playing in Wednesday and Saturday cricket with Cowdray and Petworth Town C.C.'s, and with the two clubs he took no fewer than 142 wickets at a cost of 6.3 runs each.

we all went to live at Eastern Road, Wylde Green, Sutton Coldfield, near Birmingham in Warwickshire. Experts say a baby doesn't remember anything at that age, but I do recall being wrapped in a lavender-and-white blanket with swirls on it, and being carried through the front door that had the stained-glass window set into it bearing a picture of Jesus with Joseph in his workshop.

In the late 1920s, there was a shortage of houses, and it took my father three days of camping outside our late Victorian house to secure its purchase. So, despite the fact that he liked to refer to the row of ten or so adjoining houses as "the Wylde Green Barracks" instead of calling them terraces or villas, which they were, we all knew what he had gone through to get us that house.

The United Yeast Company, one of the largest bakeries and distilleries in Birmingham, had led Father to move us to Wylde Green. Dad had

Above: Hazel's mother and father on their wedding day

accepted a job to create a recreation ground and sports club for the company. Many famous cricketers came to play there from as far away as Australia and New Zealand.

I spent hours playing with my dad on those magical fields, surrounded by beautiful bluebell woods. I fed the rabbits and birds, and rolled the turf into what we called Swiss rolls, ready for my father to resurface the cricket pitch. Dad stayed at his beloved sports ground until his retirement. To this day, I love chocolate cream Swiss roll cake, and I can't see one without being reminded of Dad's turf.

Sadly, I am sure the fields are now gone and houses built in their place.

GOLDFISH, TEA AND BOB THE MILKMAN

Life at Wylde Green rolled along for me like in a fantasy world.

Tucked away in a corner and surrounded by weeping willows, there was a lily pond. It was stocked with goldfish which I loved to catch in a small net with a long pole. I would carry them home in a large glass jam jar, and they became my friends. I enjoyed caring for them and when they died I created elaborate funerals for them, arranging flower petals in patterns down the length of our garden. These creative, ritualistic performances became the nucleus from which evolved my acting, painting, and sculpting careers.

Grandma Blockley had come to live with us, and occupied the front room so she could watch the street traffic as it unfolded during the day. At night, one could see her standing in the window, waiting for the lamplighter. She lived long enough to see the streetlights change to electricity, and would say "It is not the same. The magic is gone."

Every afternoon at 4.00, my mother and I would join her in the front room for tea with crumpets, tea cakes and homemade jam. I always sat on a little stool close to the fireplace. I was fascinated by the gaslight hanging from the centre of the room. Hanging around the light was a pink shade with a six-inch fringe made of real crystal beads. Sitting there, staring at it, I would imagine that fringe draped around my head, waist, shoulders, and neck.

Mother and I were the best of pals, and enjoyed being together. In fact, she kept me home from school six months longer than she should have, but at five years old I finally had to go.

Going to school was no hardship on me. It was wonderful fun riding to school in the milk cart, with Bob the milkman and a horse called Dobbin. Holding the reins was indescribable joy, and the clop-clop from Dobbin's

Left: Hazel's mum

hooves was music to my ears. The rich aroma of milk, and the smells of the horse and hay in the feedbag have stayed with me all these years. I remember Bob the milkman, in a moment of prescience, saying to me, "That face will be famous one day."

THE GARDEN, THE SEASONS AND MY CHESTNUT TREE

Our garden was the joy of my life. The top half belonged to my mother, and she grew flowers. She had a big flower bed and planted the same design every year. There were wallflowers in the centre, surrounded by forget-me-nots, and pansies on the outside. The bottom half of the garden belonged to my father, who grew vegetables – broad beans, French beans, cabbage, carrots, lettuce, peas, and new potatoes.

On Sundays, Mother would cook the grandest lunch with a roast of pork covered with crisp crackling fat, fresh peas, homemade apple sauce and those new potatoes cooked with fresh mint. Everything was topped off with thick brown pan gravy. The aroma of those meals could be enjoyed down the street. Just writing about it, I am getting hungry all over again.

Halfway down the garden was a wonderful swing my father built for me. Flying higher and higher, and sometimes even upside down, I performed terrifying tricks that still make me dizzy just thinking about them. At the very bottom of the garden was a chestnut tree, and that belonged to me. I would sit alone in the top branches and daydream. Under the cool canopy of its rich green leaves, I worked out everything that ever bothered me.

The tree overhung the railway station and, terrible tomboy that I was, I would sometimes hide in its dense green foliage unseen, and pelt people standing on the platform below with conkers – the outer shells of chestnuts.

Our year was very seasonal. In the spring, Father would prepare the grass for the cricket season and Mother would take me with her to bring him afternoon tea, including a Thermos of tea, watercress sandwiches and one of my favourites from my youth – homemade scones, a soothing form of food when eaten with fresh Cornish clotted cream and strawberry jam.

Spring would also bring the intoxicating perfume of wildflowers. The woods filled with bluebells, and primroses embraced the fields. We walked a lot, spending hours exploring Sutton Coldfield Park – eight miles of firs, oaks and chestnut trees surrounding four small lakes. The land was decreed to The Royal Borough of Sutton Coldfield by Henry VIII and can never be built upon or sold.

Mother would pack picnics, and we'd walk from one lake to another. The lakes have wonderful names – Windly, Powells, Bracebridge and Keepers. My love of trees began in Windly Park, my favourite because of its flocks of ducks and gorgeous beds of bulrushes.

Sometimes I hugged the trees, especially the chestnut trees. I would talk to them, and really developed a personal relationship with them. Trees give people energy, and I've always believed in their healing quality. Later in my life, the truth of this would be proven to me.

Towards the end of summer and moving into autumn, it was elderberry wine time – messy but fun. This wine was for winter when we got colds and coughs, and was served steaming hot. Dad made it rich and fruity, with pungent spices.

Autumn came as a prelude to Christmas and was always a special time in our family. In those days, we had many end-of-the-year traditions. Autumn life centred around making presents and decorations, gathering holly, mistletoe and Yule logs, and cooking festive dishes.

Our kitchen was large. As a toddler, my life seemed to revolve around the old-fashioned table which sat right in the centre of the kitchen. Not only did I eat breakfast, lunch, and dinner on that piece of furniture, and stash food I didn't care for on a little ledge on its underside, it was where I played my games and painted my pictures.

The kitchen was a warm and cosy room, full of friendly aromas, like the delicious smell of baking bread that invariably came from the oven of the big cooking range where a coal fire was always burning, or the smells of furniture polish made of beeswax and turpentine, or black lead, a substance my mother used to polish the range to a high sheen until we could see our faces reflected back to us like gray ghosts.

The second week of October would find us making Christmas cake, lightly soaked in sherry, wrapped in cotton cloth, and placed in a colourful Taylor Mincemeat tin. The third week was Christmas pudding time, and the last week was the mincemeat party. My mother prepared the mincemeat in a very large China bowl. Beside the bowl were placed silver threepenny coins, scrubbed clean. It was a tradition for all the neighbours to be invited to come by in the evening and give the mincemeat a stir.

Upon entering our house, each neighbour was given a glass of sherry and a slice of Madeira cake. As they stirred the mincemeat, they would make their wish for the coming year, and the threepenny coins would be dropped into the bowl. It was believed that the wish would come true for the lucky person who later found one of these coins in their mincemeat pie. A special loving atmosphere surrounded this occasion at the family table with its fat carved legs, covered with an old Welsh lace tablecloth from my mother's family.

I loved this night that marked the beginning of autumn as it drifted into winter. We had hot fires inside and crunchy golden leaves outside and, while it was a time when there was not a lot of money, we did have plenty of love and understanding, and Christmas stockings filled with chocolate, sweets and apples. I am so very glad to have been a part of those gentler times, and I am so grateful for two loving parents who created such special memories for me.

Three days before Christmas, we went to Sutton Coldfield Park to collect our holly and mistletoe. We stacked it on a little cart along with our Christmas log, and wheeled it home – such a simple thing but very exciting for me. Then we dressed the tree. Handed down from generation to generation, our ornaments appeared each year like old friends. I was always so happy to greet them one more time.

The day closed with a mug of hot cocoa and homemade cake. My eyes became wobbly, and images of nature's delights lulled me to sleep, happy to be alive.

LITTLE MEMORY, BIG PEONIES

In our backyard, with the flowerbed running about twenty feet to the steps leading to the garden, my mother's pride and joy were her peonies. They were beautiful flowers in every shade of pink. I watched these flowers grow and then one day, they burst into gigantic blooms.

This was too much for me. The temptation was too great. I gently snapped off every bloom and put them to rest in a basket. Then I toddled off to present them to my mother – who nearly fainted when she saw what I had done. I was in deep trouble. To this day, I see those peonies so beautiful, and have to smile.

CINDERELLA'S GLASS SLIPPERS

I was about four years old when my mother decided to take me for a holiday to Willington, a small coal-mining town in the North of England. It was near Durham, where my father had played cricket, and my parents came to live when they were first married. My mother wanted to show me off to her best friend, Annie Snowden. I couldn't say Mrs. Snowden, so she became "Mitty Snowden," a name that stuck with our family for the rest of her life.

The trip was my first long train ride. Such excitement! I've always loved trains, and this one – the London, Midland, and Scottish line – was very special. The engines in those days were wonderful, round-bellied characters puffing out clouds of pure white steam. I remember our carriage so well, with its bright red velvet seats and the little black dots all over the velvet. Over our heads, there were pink lights and a rack for our luggage made of black laced cord.

Below: Young Hazel – three years old

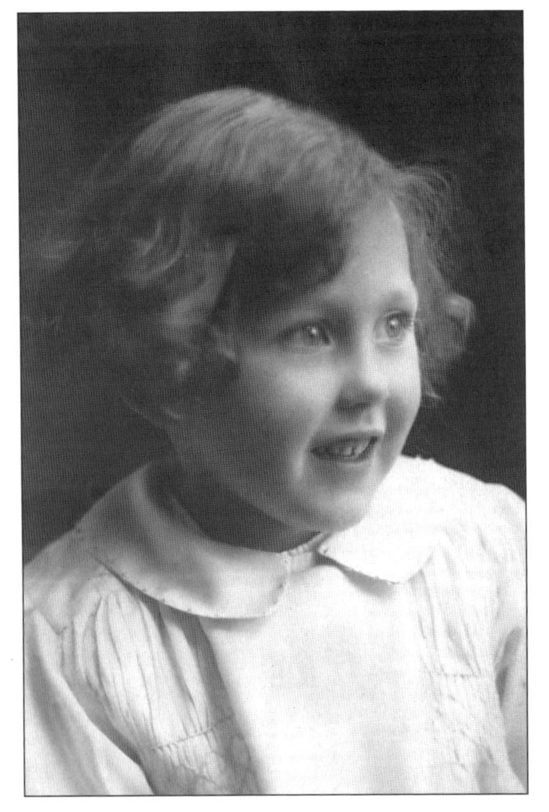

The Snowden family met us at the station, and we piled into an old taxi with Mr. and Mrs. Snowden and their three boys. I became very shy. They lived at 22 Watling Terrace – twenty-five houses built together, going down a hill. Upon our arrival, an enormous high English tea had been prepared, with lots and lots of sandwiches of ham, salmon, and watercress. There were cakes galore, and my favourite, ginger.

Annie Snowden was a love. She gave Mother and me her own room, the one she shared with Mr. Snowden, and her big strong arms carried me to bed. The bed was huge, and the mattress was made of feathers. I sank deep down. "Your mother will be up very soon, Petty." (Her "pet" name for me was "Petty, her best girl.") A big kiss, and she was gone.

My eyes were fluttering with sleep, but something across the room on the shelf above the fireplace caught my eye. It was Cinderella's glass slippers, and they were about the size of my own little foot. I scampered out of bed, pulled a little stool over to the fireplace, and grabbed the slipper. Back to bed I flew, and buried the slipper in the feathers. As I fell asleep, I was Cinderella at the ball.

Next morning, I had to get it back in its place over the fireplace. Breakfast was on its way, and I hurriedly put it under the mattress. Rushing upstairs after I had eaten my breakfast, I found and then hugged the slipper as I pulled the stool to the fireplace. As I was reaching to the ledge, the slipper fell on the tile hearth. Two pieces lay in front of me. Panic-stricken, I hid them deep under the mattress. I had been bad, and life was coming to an end.

All day I worried, and did not enjoy myself. I told Binky, the little Pekinese, the whole story. The wet runny nose and soulful eyes pored into mine. "What shall I do, Binky?" After about a minute, she sneezed all over me. I laughed and then I knew – own up.

With the two pieces in my hand, I went to Mitty Snowden and did just that. "Ah! Petty, we can glue them together," she said, "and no one will ever know. Don't you fret." Life was not over. I kissed and hugged her. That night, the moonlight touched the slipper and it glowed. No crack was to be seen. Mitty Snowden was magic.

MEMORIES LIVE LONGER THAN DREAMS: REMEMBERING VIOLET BIRD

When I was a very little girl in the 1930s, the corset lady came twice a year to see my mother. She was tiny and very thin and had no need for a corset. With her black hair swept in a bun at the nape of her neck, she was one of my favourites. Black or navy was her costume, with a stiff white shirt residing in her suit jacket and a large cameo brooch gracing her lapel. Her name was Violet Walker, but I called her Violet Bird because that is what she looked like – a bird.

My mother would show her into the living room where she would offer her coffee and cakes served on her best china. I wanted very badly to know what went on in that room, so I fixed my eye to the keyhole, which was rather large. What I saw was a cage-like contraption, kept upright with whale bones, and it was being fitted around my mother's waist. It was pink cotton with adornments of satin, metal hooks in the front, and laces down the back.

Violet Bird was pulling the laces tighter and tighter. Then I heard the bird-lady ask my mother if she felt comfortable. "Yes, yes," my mother replied, "very comfy."

I suppose after years of wearing them, the body could not be comfortable without them. My mother's figure was always slender. I'm not surprised –

considering the cage. It is hard to think of this today when bodies are falling out all over the place.

JACK FROST, QUEEN ELIZABETH AND MARIE ANTOINETTE

My bedroom had no heat. Oh yes, we had a coal fireplace, but it was only lit if one was ill. I loved Jack Frost patterns on the window, and I would trace fantasy pictures until my fingers were well on their way to frostbite. My mother thought it was healthy to sleep in a cold room. Thinking back, I find it hard to believe. If we complained, she had an extraordinary saying. She would tell us, "A warm room will make you nesh." Nesh means "soft, tender, or delicate," but at the time, we had no idea where that word came from. My sister and I shared a room, and as we grew older, we never felt the cold, so obviously Mother was right. We never did become nesh.

From the word "go," I wanted to be an actress. I sang and acted out stories on top of the bed, going into my mother's bedroom, and taking the eiderdown quilt to tie around my waist for my costume. I would make myself look like a character from the 17th century and pretend I was Queen Elizabeth I or Marie Antoinette. Everyone knew when I was going to sleep because at bedtime I would sing "God Save the Queen." My sister's clothes also came in very handy at times like those. One time I made my mother very cross when I devoured about a pound of Macintosh toffees, twisted the colourful papers into butterflies, and stuck them onto the ceiling as set dressing for my show that night. There was no question as to what I was going to do when I grew up.

Every week on Friday night, we would go to the cinema. It was a ritual. There were big crowds, and we always had to wait in line. Deanna Durbin, Astaire and Rogers, Joan Crawford, John Wayne – I was in awe of all of them. On the way home from the movies, I would always walk behind my parents, and Mother said I acted out all the parts behind their backs. "My God, George, she remembers all the lines," she would say to my father. Those were golden days, standing in line to get into the movies.

Sometimes we would walk three miles to a cinema called the Pavilion. Other times we would go to the Odeon. In the intermission, up from the ground would come this giant organ. Then it would sink back into the ground. Of course, I was fascinated, and my imagination took off. I also remember the lights around the curtain – arches of amber, reds and yellows.

At Christmastime, Mother always had a stall at the Christmas fair, where twenty little booths in the village hall were packed together like sardines. Everybody knew each other and worked together. In our stall, we had everything from baby clothes to strawberry jam.

Decorating the church was a special time, with holly and ivy caressing the giant pillars, while red and white flowers adorned the altar.

On the altar steps, there was a crib with the baby Jesus inside, lying on cascading straw. The pulpit was smothered in fir and mistletoe, and I always thought it looked as if it was wearing its winter coat and getting a little overheated. At the end of the day, there would be a show put on by the church.

Religion was never pushed on me, but was always available. I loved going to church with my Mother, Father, and Grandma Blockley. With her fascinating hats, in either maroon or black with mounds of velvet, Grandma was very stately and looked like the old Queen Mary. Walking into church with her made me feel very proud. Feathers in her hats were kept in place with a beautiful diamond pin, and her throat was always covered in lace. On either side of her throat, little whalebones kept the lace in place.

We attended the Protestant Church – the Church of England. The joy of going every Sunday and becoming very much part of the Church is still with me. I always managed to get in the church show somewhere, as a fairy or a flowerpot. Standing on the stage, looking out across the audience, I remember the feelings that came over me, feelings of importance, power, independence, and make-believe. The stage bug had bitten me, well and truly. Sometimes I'm staggered by my memory of so long ago. It all made a very lasting impression on me.

Later on, when I grew up a bit, I was chosen to play the archangel Gabriel in the nativity play. I wore white wings on my head. I was to rise from the pulpit, but they didn't give me a proper platform to rise from – it was only two cushions on top of each other. The cushions tipped and I fell over but, just like Jesus, the Angel Gabriel rose again.

This was the true beginning of my acting career. I was so proud of myself.

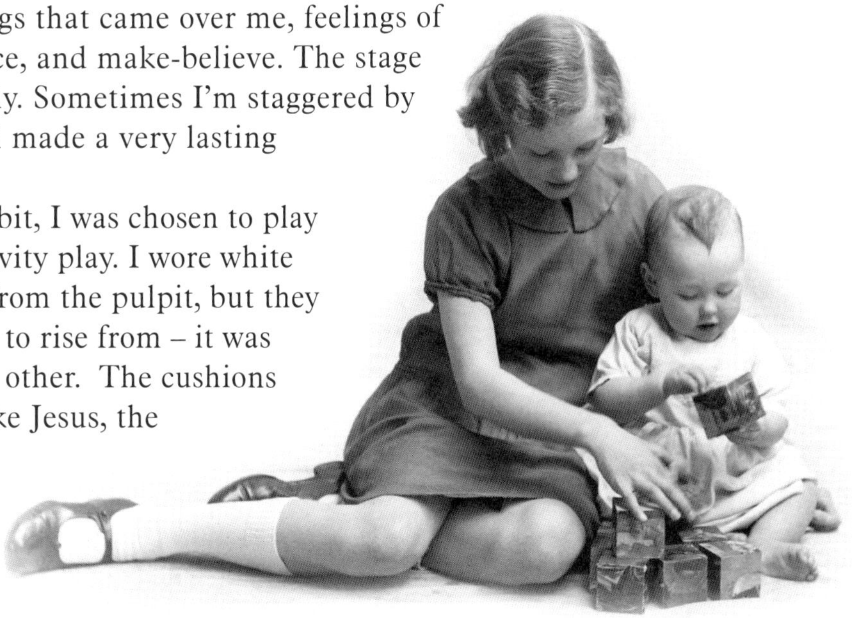

Hazel (right) and sister Audrey, 1926

Then, as I got older, at Boldmere Church, I played the Virgin Mary with a beautiful blue veil tied under the chin. I was the cat's whiskers. It would be many, many years before I would visit Boldmere Church again, with many wonderful performances in between.

PEACE IN OUR TIME

Some misconception of the world made me think this idyllic life would go on forever. Such things, as we all know, are never really possible. There was much whispering going on between Mother and Father, and they looked worried all the time. I sensed an aura of change in the air. The radio was turned on many times during the day and my father was forever running out to top up the accumulator battery that ran the radio.

One day when the radio was on, I heard my father calling my mother.

"Madge! Madge! It's going to be okay. Chamberlain is back and it's all going to be worked out. Peace in our time."

"What does that mean?" I asked my father.

He told me, "There is not going to be a war."

The phrase, "Peace in our time" had come from the Prime Minister of the UK at the time, Neville Chamberlain. He had been in Germany and, when he returned, he had gotten off the plane, held up his hand and said "Everything is going to be okay. Peace in our time."

War, the word of darkness. I did not fully understand what it meant until the next day when I arrived at school to find labourers hard at work bulldozing the playground. When I found out that fun and games were about to be replaced by concrete bunkers, I got a glimpse of what was to come.

Peace in our time was a myth, but it did give us a year to prepare. Up until then, the only weapon we had for fighting a war was our guts – and war was on its way. Soon, planes were built and ammunition factories established. I may have only been thirteen years old, but I was unafraid and ready to do whatever had to be done. One year later in 1939, Britain declared war on Germany. At school we had air raid warning drills, and at home my father became an air raid warden.

We lived not far from Birmingham and Coventry, where there were many ammunition factories, making us a prime target area for the Nazi bombs. Our next door neighbours told us we were going to be sharing an Anderson shelter, a small corrugated-iron construction, shaped like a beehive and sitting half below ground and half above. The shelter was erected at the bottom of the

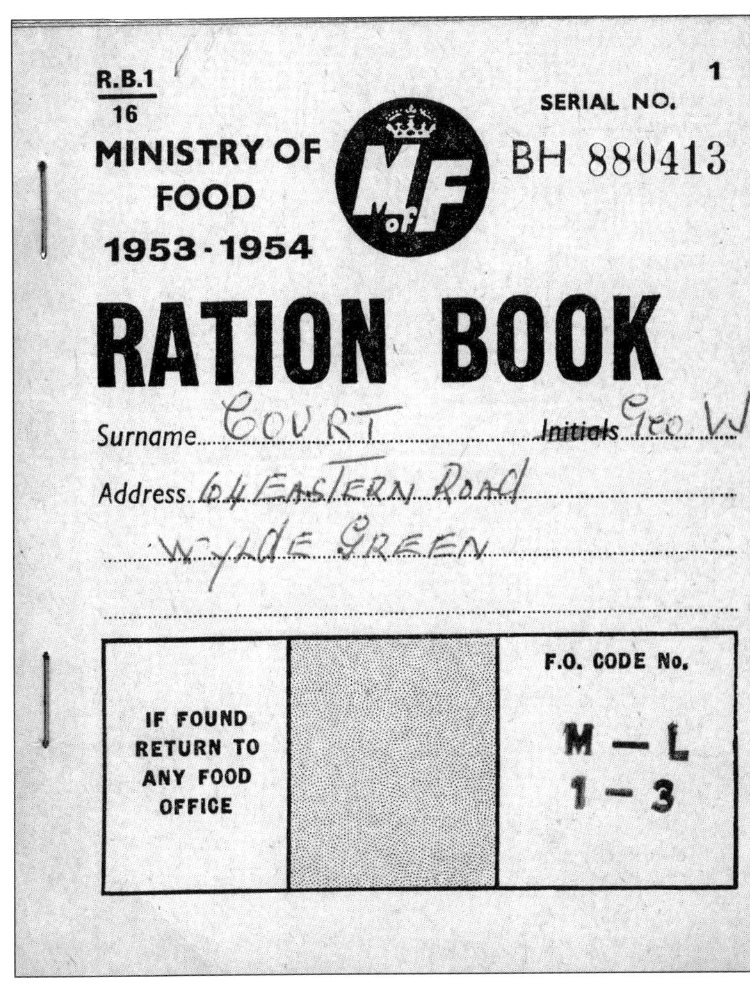
R.B.1
16
1
MINISTRY OF FOOD
1953-1954
SERIAL NO.
BH 880413

RATION BOOK

Surname COURT Initials Geo W
Address 64 EASTERN ROAD
WYLDE GREEN

IF FOUND RETURN TO ANY FOOD OFFICE		F.O. CODE No. M — L 1 — 3

Left: Hazel at thirteen years old

Right: War Ration Book – 1953-1954

garden under my beloved chestnut tree. Some time would elapse before we would actually use the shelter but when we did, we would spend hours in it drinking hot cocoa and tea, hugging hot water bottles to keep us warm. It was built to hold six people sitting on each side, but we often had more. Around 5.30 in the evening, we would go into the shelter, and leave at 5.30 the following morning when the Germans had finished their bombing raids.

Grandma Blockley was the first to appear when the sirens started to wail. She would be right there, hugging her blanket and Thermos flask, a white baby shawl – Aunt Annie's, maybe? – wrapped around her head in place of her velvet toque. My mother and I were always the last to get out of bed. One night, after a very large bomb exploded nearby, we collided at the top of the stairs and almost took the trip from top to bottom together.

November 14, 1940, the night Coventry was nearly bombed out of existence, will always be in my memory. We were in the shelter by 5.00 p.m. The drone of German bombs started immediately and continued through to the next morning. The sky was pink at first, and then turned blood red, and I remember everybody saying, "Somebody's getting it tonight – and it looks like Coventry."

The strangest thing was, I never really felt afraid. I knew I was not going to die in an Anderson shelter under my dear friend, the chestnut tree. But many did die, and I salute their memory on these pages.

I lost friends in the war, but I did not grieve for them until later. "When we have won," my father would say to me, "then you can cry for your friends. For now, we must be strong and stick together."

During the war we had very little food. A ration of three pieces of bacon, one ounce of butter, and one ounce of sugar – this would have to last for a month. Rabbit, spam and sardines were a large part of our diet. We had no bananas or oranges, and eggs were like gold.

I was thirteen years old when the War began, and I became a War teenager. My sister married a handsome squadron leader in the Royal Air Force. My lovely niece Victoria was born during an air raid. I was the first to hold her. In spite of the War, the family was healthy, all hanging together.

Eventually, tragedy would strike. It would come later, in 1944, after I made the film *Champagne Charlie*. My sister's husband would die on his Air Force base in Northern England. He was involved in the business of decoys – dummy planes replacing the real ones to fool the Germans. One day on the decoy site, he would be walking across the base while an air raid and thunderstorm were happening simultaneously. Upon reaching his office, he would collapse and die. We would never really know what happened.

It would be my first experience of death in the family, and I would take it very badly. I loved my sister and niece, so I would go to live with them in Ealing, just outside of London, in a charming Georgian house.

As I write about these memories of fifty-something years ago, I am sitting in an exquisite garden in Provence, France. The Hotel de la Pouche, built hundreds of years ago as a small castle, is magnificent. Peace reigns supreme. It is a magical day, and I am visited by frogs, lizards, and dragonflies. Vineyards and, of course, lavender fields surround me.

In the 1940s, and earlier still during the French Revolution, wars raged over this land. Today, only jets – very, very noisy – disturb the air. At least they are not guns or bombs.

EVACUATION

One day at Boldmere School, I was called to the office of Miss Barton the headmistress and asked to be seated and wait for her. I thought I had done something wrong. Eventually, Miss Barton appeared and introduced me to a gentleman. I don't remember his name, but he was from the British Evacuation Board. He told me I had been chosen for evacuation to Durban, South Africa, and said I would need to undergo a medical examination and interview.

I was stunned beyond belief. "Do my parents know?"

"Not yet," Miss Barton replied.

The interview was to take place the next day, along with a physical exam which included an inspection of my teeth and hair.

"You can go home now," Miss Barton said, handing me a letter to give to my parents.

Where we lived, bombing was very bad. Many of my friends were being evacuated out to the country or to the United States, but this was different. I believe one special student was chosen from each of the Boldmere area schools, and other students were chosen from the rest of the country.

I had good but not outstanding grades, and I was good at a number of other things like art, gymnastics, ballet, and sports. I was popular with the other children. My body was strong, my teeth were perfect, and I had great hair. They were looking for what I call "all-rounders."

I handed the letter to my parents, and explained what it was all about. They were very quiet.

"Your father and I must discuss this together, in private, darling" my mother said, her voice strained. "It's a very serious commitment."

I waited for a long while, wondering about the situation in which I found myself. Finally my parents appeared.

"How do you feel about going so far away from home?" my mother asked.

"Well, I am very interested," I replied, "but at the same time, I'm worried about leaving you and Daddy."

"We feel it's an honour for you to have been chosen," my father responded with a soft and gentle voice, "and if you are happy about it, we will give our permission."

The next day, I was tested North, South, East, and West. They concluded that I was an excellent specimen of youth, and I was accepted for this giant evacuation plan. We were allowed only one not-too-large suitcase per student. Numerous label tags were required, some for around my wrists and neck, and one

I will never forget that went on my suitcase. It was a giant label in bright yellow with black letters, which read "Great Britain Evacuation Board." I was on my way.

Life had done a cartwheel for me – and for my parents who were wonderful, never letting me see how upset they were to be parting with me. It was for my own good. Daddy kept telling me it wouldn't be for long. The war would soon be over. I believed him, and thought it was just going to be a holiday to an orange farm in South Africa. The day came for all of us to say goodbye. My sister came to the station with my parents. We all hugged and hugged, kissed and kissed. Those terrible words, "It won't be for long", kept being repeated.

Families were to go to Birmingham New Street Station, bound for Glasgow, Scotland. There we would board the big ship called *The Llandaff Castle*. Suddenly it was a big adventure. Looking back, I can't believe Mum and Dad let me go. We were a very close, loving family.

Somewhere a whistle blew. I was hurried into a compartment with a bunch of girls. Through the window, I waved goodbye. My mother was crying, I was crying, and it seemed the whole world was crying. Images flashed across my mind, of home, chestnut trees and my wonderful grandmother. I was on my way to the unknown land of oranges. The girls were all very nice and friendly, but they all looked stunned, as I know I did.

Hours later, we arrived in Glasgow and were taken to a school where we were to spend the night before boarding ship. Mattresses were laid in the great hall where we would sleep, head to toe, toe to head. I remember something strange. We all had autograph books and got everybody in sight to sign them. I laugh when I think of it now.

The next day came and went, and then the next, and we were still on the floor in the school. It was a whole week before we actually boarded the ship. We were anchored off the coast of Scotland on the large and tremendous ship *The Llandaff Castle*. Finally it was all coming true.

The girls in my group were fifteen and sixteen, a year or two older than me. They were all in love with a very handsome purser, and the endless preening that went on fascinated me. Makeup appeared from nowhere, and padded bras were the fashion of the day. Ankle socks were discarded and black lines were drawn on the back of the legs where the seams of the stockings would have been had there been any. Still wearing white ankle socks and black patent leather shoes, I found this all very interesting. We were all growing up fast, and having fun doing it. Even a few air raids didn't seem to bother us. Boys had boarded the ship and there was great excitement.

Days were going by and no sailing was happening. It all seemed a little ominous. Then one day, we were summoned to the big dining area. We were told that the fighting on the North African Coast had become very intense, and German submarines were everywhere.

"I am sad to inform you," said the Captain, "that we are going to have to return to Glasgow. Once there, we will await further instructions."

"But, why?" we all wanted to know.

"I'm sorry," he explained, "but it has become too dangerous to take you children across the ocean."

So we disembarked, and the next day, before we knew what was happening, we were put on the train for home. Each and all the girls promised to keep in touch and write, but we were all like deflated balloons. The train chugged into the station in Birmingham, and we were all hanging out the windows to find our families at the barriers. It was a great moment, just like in the film *Hope and Glory*. Screaming and yelling, everybody rushed forward, breaking the barriers. I saw my mother and flew into her arms. She cried. I cried. The whole world cried together. We were home. Let the bombs fall. We would survive. We were home with our families, vowing never to leave again.

I only actually kept in touch with one girl for a couple of years. It was a strange time in my life, an episode suspended somewhere in space off the coast of Scotland. Towards the end of the war *The Llandaff Castle* was sunk. Rest in peace, dear ship.

MY FIRST LOVE

He tipped his face up a little as very gently, raindrops began to fall. The very low gaslight softly lit his golden curls. Water caressed his face and highlighted his handsome cheekbones. I loved his face and the wicked boyish grin that went with it. He was seventeen, and a heartbreaker. I was fifteen, and there was no doubt about it, I was madly in love.

For weeks, I had watched him riding his bicycle around my neighbourhood. My own bicycle was not the best in the world. It had a permanent wobble in the front wheel but, in early 1940, I was lucky to have a bicycle. We still did not comprehend what was coming.

One typically damp English afternoon, I was riding home from school when I rounded a corner at an angle my bicycle did not enjoy, and I was thrown over the handlebars. My chin hit the ground, followed by the rest of me. Badly stunned, I lifted up my head, and through a million stars, I saw

Right: Hazel at fifteen years old, from the photo shoot that launched Hazel's career – Taken by J.W. (by gaslight)

that Heaven had come to earth. J.W. was there, very close, holding me in his arms. Nothing else in the whole world mattered. Love had left the starting gate and was headed for the winning post.

My hair was red and very long. My eyes were Welsh green and large. His eyes were blue. Oh, those eyes – penetrating Saxon blue. Speeding around on our bicycles, those golden chariots, we painted a lovely picture. Our bicycles took us everywhere, through woods and down country lanes, along those fairytale English streams and little rivers. There, we would lie on the cool banks, holding each other with a strange energy, exchanging kisses that made one tipsy. We talked of many things – our families, school, what we would like to achieve in our lives – but never, ever about the War.

There was always a faraway aura about him, powerful and unapproachable. After a very loving moment, he would often say, "Time to go, H.C." (his nickname for me), and before I knew it, he was gone. It did no good to question or argue. In 1940, no one questioned anyone. We just accepted things.

Each afternoon we would meet after school and bicycle to the local teashop. Once there, we could always be found munching the same cakes. His was "Squashed flies," a flaky pastry full of currants. Mine was a round sponge cake covered in pink icing, and held together by a strip of paper dotted with gold hearts. How appropriate. Those were golden hours set in golden days, etched in my mind forever.

Usually I would find J.W. smoking a cigarette, but on this one particular night he was standing very still, waiting for me. "Come on, H.C.," he said, taking my hand. "Let's go to the old railway bridge." We had spent many hours there, giggling and laughing, loving the thunderous sound of the trains. As we perched on the wall, I suddenly felt a horrible silence, the kind that always has a bad ending.

He held me very tight, and I knew something had happened.

"H.C., I have something to tell you."

My heart was pounding like the trains overhead.

"I've joined the Merchant Navy. I leave in two days time," he said, a faraway look in his eyes.

"Why? Why? Why?" I sobbed.

"Because I've been called up and there's nothing I can do about it." He had volunteered, and then got called up right away.

That horrible foreboding silence had indeed had a bad ending, and there was nothing I could do about it either. He pulled me up toward him and kissed me hard, with great passion.

"I'll walk you home." His words came out like bullets.

My house was not very far, and we stopped short of the gate, under a tree. A light rain was beginning to fall, creating an eerie mist. His hand went into his blazer, and he pulled out a small packet, handing it to me.

"I want you to have this. It's my badge from high school, telling the world I'm a very clever boy and got top marks." A short laugh escaped from both of us.

And then he said, "I don't think I'll be seeing you again, H.C., but I love you with all my heart. Go and become a famous actress and make all those movies you talk about. I'll be watching from the stalls. Remember me. And remember our year together."

Once again he was gone. It was almost as if he had never been there. Like the curtain at the end of a play, the rain was now coming down heavily. I was numb. My feet were frozen to the pavement. I couldn't move. Somewhere in the mist and rain, my first love was running off to sea, hurting, hurting. His ship was sunk in the North Atlantic in 1941. There were no survivors.

J.W. was very important in my early life. Not only was he my first love, but just for fun, he had taken photographs of me by gaslight, and those very same photographs later brought me into films. He was a role model for strength of character, and for bravery. This unselfish young warrior would have surely found peace in death. I am sure his soul was taken to Heaven on the arm of the Lord. Perhaps the golden memories of our love went with him. I know the memory of his bicycle did.

CHAMPAGNE CHARLIE

I had given my sister Audrey a batch of the photographs J.W. had taken of me. She carried them in her wallet. One fateful day at the Midland Hotel in Manchester, she and her husband – who was working with the UK's Counter-Intelligence and Security Agency, MI5 – were having cocktails with Sir Anthony Asquith and Mr. Norman Loudon.

Sir Anthony Asquith was the son of H.H. Asquith, who served as Prime Minister of the United Kingdom from 1908-1916. Above and beyond being from a well-known family, Asquith was highly esteemed as a film director, and was instrumental in forming the London Film Society to promote artistic appreciation of film. In the 1920s he spent some time in Hollywood, and then returned to England to become a film director.

Pygmalion (1938) is one of Asquith's best known films. He co-directed the film with its star, Leslie Howard, and the film was nominated in the States for several Academy Awards. George Bernard Shaw – with whom Asquith co-founded the London Film Society – won the Oscar for Best Adapted Screenplay.

Loudon was a very impressive Scotsman, and the owner of Shepperton Studios, a film studio in Shepperton, Middlesex. Loudon, best known for a 1934 drama entitled *Designing Women*, had worked with many fine actors and made a number of excellent films.

As they all sat there chatting and enjoying their drinks, Audrey reached into her wallet for something, and as luck would have it, the photographs of me accidentally fell to the floor. Anthony Asquith picked them up and glanced at them as he was handing them back to my sister.

"Who is the girl in the pictures? She is very pretty. She should be in films," he said.

Norman Loudon looked at the photographs and was also intrigued.

"Why, that is my sister Hazel," Audrey responded.

Before I knew it, it was arranged that my mother would accompany me as I travelled from Birmingham where I lived to London, to be interviewed by Margaret Bonner, the head of casting at Ealing Studios.

Taking over the site formerly occupied by Will Barker Studios, Associated Talking Pictures reopened the studio as Ealing Studios in 1931. Over the years, the studio would change hands and issue films not only under the Ealing Studios moniker but as Associated Talking Pictures and the Rank Organisation as well. Earning a reputation for its celebrated, often lightly satirical comedies, the studio produced scores of popular films, including *Champagne Charlie*. Some became classics, like *Passport to Pimlico*, *Whisky Galore, The Man in the White Suit, The Ladykillers,* and *the Lavender Hill Mob*.

Owing to his several Ealing performances, including a dark comedy *Kind Hearts and Coronets*, Alec Guinness – already a theatrical success – became a huge star.

In addition to their comedies, Ealing Studios became known for their war films distinguished by their dedication to realism, and was one of only three British studios to continue production throughout World War II. Their war films emphasised the contributions of ordinary men and women of all classes and regions, united in the fight against a common enemy.

Opposite Page: Hazel at fifteen years old, from the photo shoot that launched Hazel's career – Taken by J.W. (by gaslight)

Right: Hazel at sixteen years old, first professional photo session for Champagne Charlie (1944)

Opposite page
Top: A poster for Bond Street

Bottom: Poster, Champagne Charlie (1944)

Now you know a bit about Ealing Studios, where Margaret Bonner was the head of casting. As it turned out, she was a charming lady and put me at great ease. Thankfully, I was not entirely without experience, as I had been in *School for Scandal* at the Birmingham Alexander Theatre and also a play called *Pack up Your Troubles*, and had passed with high marks when I took my acting exams at the London Academy of Music.

She told me about a very, very small part not yet cast in a film called *Champagne Charlie*. It seemed she wanted a certain type of face and I was that face. I got the part and returned to London, without my mother this time.

The movie, named for singer George Leybourne, was a splendid story of the British Music Halls of the 1860s. The title song, "Champagne Charlie," was first performed by Leybourne in 1867. One of the brightest stars of the golden age of music hall, Leybourne is said to have been paid a salary by Moët to appear in public dressed immaculately, drinking nothing but champagne, earning himself the nickname "Champagne Charlie."

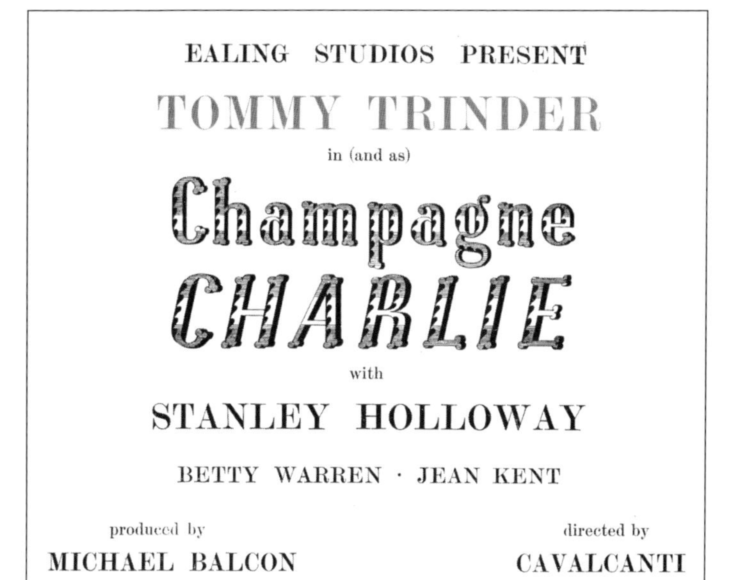

The picture starred Stanley Holloway, Betty Warren, Jean Kent and one of England's great comics, Tommy Trinder. A few years later, I would be in another film with Jean Kent, and we would become friendly. That film was called *Bond Street*, and in it I wear the most beautiful wedding dress you've ever seen.

In *Champagne Charlie*, dramatic tension is provided by the rivalry between George "Champagne Charlie" Leybourne, played by Tommy Trinder, and Alfred Peck "The Great Vance" Stevens, played by Holloway, best known for his song "Walking in the Zoo". The Great Vance was a stylish rake who carried a gold-knobbed cane, wore an eyeglass, and died on stage in 1889 during a Boxing Day performance at the Sun Music Hall in Knightsbridge.

Above Top: Sir Anthony Asquith

Above Bottom: Some early theatrical experience in Pack up Your Troubles helped prepare Hazel (bottom right) for a career in films

The first lines I ever spoke in a film were in *Champagne Charlie*, when I said "I've never had champagne before and I love it. I think I'm getting tipsy."

While working on *Champagne Charlie* (1944), I was staying at a hotel in Ealing. Nearby, bombs were dropping. A particularly deadly bomb went off. It was called a Bread Basket for its ability to throw out other bombs as it hit the ground – one of which landed near my hotel. Most of the windows in the hotel shattered, but I was determined not to let even Hitler or the War stop my film debut.

Being on a film set for the first time, and knowing my film career was beginning, was a dream coming true. I remembered those early days of walking behind Mother and Father after we had been to a movie, acting out all the parts and reciting the dialogue, and now here I was actually in a film. I even had two lines. Nothing would ever top that first day.

Tommy Trinder was fascinating and became one of England's greatest comics. In a strange coincidence, Trinder actually first appeared onstage at Collins Music Hall in Islington which is where George Leybourne made "Champagne Charlie" famous almost eighty years before.

While Nazi bombs were still falling all over London, Tommy Trinder's breezy cockney patter on BBC Radio, and his sharp sense of fun, helped people all over Britain escape their worries and the nightly horrors of the Blitz. Watching him act, I was mesmerised. With his arms and legs always on the go, he was in constant motion. He was a charming and lovable character, and a very funny man. I remember being introduced to him.

"Blimey, what big eyes you've got," he said.

"The better to see you with," I replied. I don't know what I was thinking. Was I already too big for my boots?

I only had half a day's work and two lines, yet it felt like it was all meant to be. It seemed like I was on an extraordinary path that I never thought would not happen. Defeat was never a thought in my mind.

Betty Warren, a larger-than-life lady, was marvellous as Bessie Bellwood, a big-busted, larger-than-life character. I never did meet Stanley Holloway on *Champagne Charlie*. It wasn't until a few years later that I met him when I was working on *Carnival* and he was playing my father in the film. These characters created tremendous energy, and it was all terribly exciting.

Alberto Cavalcanti, the celebrated Brazilian director with a love of melodrama and a background in *avant garde* and documentary realism, was marvellous.

Above Left: Terry Bishop, Victoria Barton, Audrey, Sally Walsh and Hazel at the wedding of Audrey and Terry Bishop

Above Right: Terry Bishop, Hazel and Audrey at the wedding of Audrey and Terry Bishop

The film was a success. Even I – with my two little lines delivered from the balcony of an old Music Hall Theatre – received good notices for my performance.

Vernon Greeves, my boyfriend in the film, took me to opening night. I was so excited, and couldn't believe I would get such good reviews for only two lines. I was on a high, and on my way to a movie career – large or small, it didn't matter to me. I was hooked.

Sometimes I think life has all happened before and we are on a rerun. The feeling of *déjà vu* has often been with me.

DREAMING

I lost my heart to Norman Loudon, the fascinating Scotsman who had started me on the road to fame when he picked up my gaslight photographs after they fell from my sister's handbag. Serendipity seemed to follow Loudon. In fact, it was a chance meeting with Loudon that brought director John Baxter to Sound City Studios at Shepperton.

Loudon was charming, powerful, very worldly-wise – and forty years old. I was seventeen. It was 1944, not long after *Champagne Charlie*, and we were making *Dreaming* at Loudon's Shepperton Studios.

The studio had always fascinated me, thanks in no small part to Paul Robeson, the great African-American singer who had made *Sanders of the River* there in 1935. The film had been a major part of my growing up, and

Paul Robeson's mystical voice was a permanent part of my memory. Some of you may not know who he is but there's never been anyone like him before or since. He was a magical human being.

Dreaming starred Flanagan and Allen, Britain's top comic act. They laughed, told jokes together, fooled around, and sang – their signature tune was "Underneath the Arches," and I think the arches referred to Friar Gate railway bridge in Derby. They made everybody adore them. They were England's best-loved comics by far.

The War was not yet over. The odd bomb was still falling. Still, working on *Dreaming* was quite a great experience for me. Everyone on the picture teased the life out of me, and I laughed from beginning to end. In one scene, I played an exotic native girl with brown makeup all over my body. They loved to dribble water on the makeup to make it run. They were such wonderful people, one forgave them anything. As delightful as it was to make *Dreaming*, it was also difficult because, as I said, I was madly in love with the owner of the studio.

Loudon was a big businessman who drank wonderful whisky and wines. He also smoked the very best cigars, and the smoke got into my long red hair which then needed to be washed continuously. He was full of fun, and he

This Page and Opposite: Hazel with Flanagan and Allen and various cast of Dreaming (1945)

laughed a lot. He was one big Scottish handful. He was my first affair, and I was crazy about him. On *Dreaming*, I had to cope not only with Flanagan and Allen but with a Scottish Laird!

Norman was taking me to wonderful places, and introducing me to excellent wines, and my eyes were out on organ stops. Because the war was still on, at night we would go down into the air raid shelters. The affair with Norman continued, and we were really very close. Then one day, thanks to studio gossip, I discovered there was another woman tucked away in the Scottish Highlands. She was very beautiful, with black hair, black eyes and alabaster skin. Her name was Maggie, and she had been Norman's secretary for many years.

One day she came to the Studios, and I was asked to meet her in the study of the old house. She was friendly and very gracious, but I could not understand what message she was trying to convey to me until she said, "If you ever need to talk to me, I will be there for you." Suddenly, everything became clear to me. I knew in my heart that she had probably been Loudon's mistress for years, and I could tell that she wanted to talk to me more deeply. Even though the conversation did not go that way, still I got the message.

Norman was in a difficult spot, torn by his love for both his Scottish beauty and his eighteen-year-old redhead who was full of life and adventure. He was besotted with me. I believe Maggie would have removed herself to Scotland, but I knew that staying with him wasn't the right thing. The whole situation had almost bounced out of control, and I knew what I had to do.

Below: Hazel with Flanagan and Allen in Dreaming (1945)

It was up to me to make it right. Saying goodbye was hard, but the only way to go. If we had stayed together, I could have owned Shepperton Studios, but instead I did the right thing, asking only that Norman build covered walkways to the dressing rooms and sound stages.

Several years later, I returned to Shepperton Studios to make *Devil Girl from Mars* (1954), and I saw that he had done what I asked. The studio had been golden. Norman and Maggie were in the Highlands. Everything was in its place.

GAIETY GEORGE

In 1946 came *Gaiety George*. Strangely, like *Champagne Charlie*, this film was also about the music halls of the 1860s.

The film was produced and directed by George King, the famous producer/director who was the power of the British Theatre of the late 1800s. He was very handsome and articulate, not at all old school. He was verging on a modern day American producer/director. His wife Connie King would survive him and go on to marry a famous plastic surgeon who I would encounter peripherally later on in my career – Sir Archibald McIndoe.

The film starred Richard Greene and Ann Todd. Greene would later become famous as Robin Hood but was then known as "the Brylcreem Boy." Brylcreem was a product used to slick down men's hair and make it shine, and it did just that. In fact, it made men's hair look like the shine my mother would get on her grate after using black lead polish.

Richard was so good looking and photogenic. He was also a good actor but, as so often happens, he became famous mostly for his looks. His wife, Patricia Medina, the British actress, became a dear friend of mine. Pat was also a great beauty. She had those large, dark Spanish eyes and coal black hair to her waist. When I first met them together, I could do nothing but stare.

Later, Pat would marry Joseph Cotten, an American actor who was good friends with my second husband, American actor/director Don Taylor. Joe was a wonderful and gracious human being, and I remember him with great love. He possessed elegance and manners rarely seen today. The mould has been broken.

Gaiety George was a tremendous success and great fun to make. Ann Todd, a lovely actress, was a big hit and went on to make *The Seventh Veil* with James Mason, a film considered a classic today.

As for me, I had only a single line. Replying to a question about what I did in life, I said, "I do embroidery, Sir." My one line got me a couple of good reviews and an audition for *Carnival,* a musical.

CARNIVAL

Carnival (1946) was written and produced by Compton MacKenzie, and starred Michael Wilding, Stanley Holloway and Sally Gray. Without a doubt one of England's most gorgeous actresses, Gray was blonde, with brown eyes and a sexy downturn of her mouth. She made her name in the film *Dangerous Moonlight.* I loved that movie. It featured Anton Walbrook of *The Red Shoes* fame and had that wonderful Warsaw Concerto by Richard Addinsell. It was a very stirring piece.

The film was set in Penzance, Cornwall, and we were all on location there for six months. Filming in Cornwall began my lifelong love for that part

This page and opposite: Publicity shots for Carnival (1946)

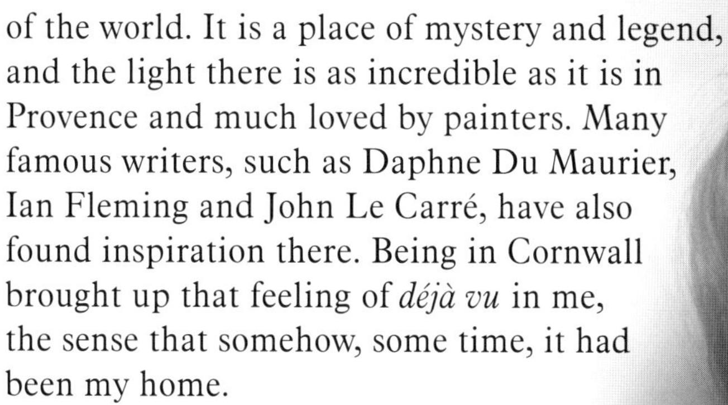

of the world. It is a place of mystery and legend, and the light there is as incredible as it is in Provence and much loved by painters. Many famous writers, such as Daphne Du Maurier, Ian Fleming and John Le Carré, have also found inspiration there. Being in Cornwall brought up that feeling of *déjà vu* in me, the sense that somehow, some time, it had been my home.

It was one of those locations where people fell in and out of love and where marriages were made or split. That was definitely the case for Michael Wilding and Sally Gray, who were very much in love by the end of the picture. They would stay together for a number of years and later, after they parted, Michael would go on to marry Elizabeth Taylor.

I landed the very interesting part of a young disabled girl in the film. In the part, the girl had a club foot. I was so excited, I thought I would burst. Stanley Holloway played my father, and Catherine Lacey was my mother. Stanley was a lovable dad and a great storyteller. Bernard Miles was a big joke teller. He wrote down the day's jokes in a little book he kept with him, and he was always pinching my behind. Today, he would have gotten in a lot of trouble for that! Then we just laughed and carried on.

Stanley Haynes was the director, and

Guy Green was the cameraman. Guy had photographed *Great Expectations* and *Oliver Twist* for director David Lean. Guy was a brilliant cinematographer but he had plenty of talent to give, and wanted more from the film world than what he could find as a cameraman. He turned to directing and had an enormous hit with *The Angry Silence* with Richard Attenborough. It was a very wonderful film.

Guy followed that success with *The Mark* starring Stuart Whitman and Rod Steiger. Whitman won the Oscar for Best Actor in a Leading Role, and Guy Green was nominated for a Golden Palm at the Cannes Film Festival. The film also won the Samuel Goldwyn Award for Best English Film of 1962. The film led Guy to Hollywood where he directed *A Patch of Blue* with Sidney Poitier, Elizabeth Hartman and Shelley Winters. The film got several award nominations, and Shelley Winters won the Oscar for Best Supporting Actress. It also earned Guy a Writer's Guild of America nomination for Best Written American Drama (1966). *Light in the Piazza* followed for Guy, along with many more successes.

I had always been very close to both Guy and his wife, Jo, who still lives in Hollywood, and was heart-broken when I had heard that Guy had passed on in 2005 after a long and undeserved illness. But his one giant leap from Cornwall to California had certainly been well worth the effort.

The hotel where we stayed in Penzance had been used by the forces in the War. Although it had been cleaned,

This page and opposite: Publicity shots for Carnival (1946)

the fleas remained, and we all got bitten very badly. All the mattresses and bed linens had to be removed. Eventually the flea festival was over.

Overall, our stay in Penzance proved to be quite an experience and, on the night of the Allied Forces' victory over Japan, we celebrated all night long with dancing in the streets.

THE RANK ORGANISATION

It was August of 1945 and a mushroom-shaped cloud marked the first wartime use of the bomb and the destruction of Hiroshima. Somehow the world travelled on, but my mind never felt settled on the subject of that bomb. So many were obliterated in a second. I know many people say, "Yes, but so many were saved by the bomb, too." It was such a horrendous moment that I have never come together over it one way or the other. It is easy to say that wars are wrong until soldiers are marching up your garden with guns raised to shoot you.

Next came the stories of the concentration camps. At first we didn't believe them, but slowly the horror became reality. Many years later, while filming *Jack of Diamonds* in Munich, Germany, my second husband, Don Taylor, would take me to Dachau Concentration Camp. The Germans made the camp into a museum and, to their credit, they did it very well, sparing themselves nothing. The day of our visit is one I will never forget, and it made such an impact on us that it was quite a few days before we could talk normally to each other. They say that no birds ever fly over Dachau. Certainly, neither Don nor I saw any.

The War came to an end, and in 1946, my agent told me of rumours of a contract with the J. Arthur Rank Organisation. The company was formed to keep British film industry interests in England. Prior to World War II, eighty percent of British screen time was occupied by American films, but by 1942, the Rank Organisation owned 619 cinemas.

I was asked to test for them. Of course I agreed, and was sent to be interviewed by Michael Powell and Emeric Pressburger, the wonderful team

Above: Producer/director Michael Powell and Hazel representing Rank at the Argentina Film Festival

Right: An early autograph session for Rank

Left: Michael Powell, Janet Munro and Hazel at the Argentina Film Festival

that gave us *The Life and Death of Colonel Blimp* and many more. Halfway through the interview, I heard them whispering to each other, saying that I was perfect for *The Red Shoes*, their next film.

"Do you dance, Miss Court?" asked Mr. Powell.

"Well, yes," I said, "I was trained in ballet before I became an actress."

"Good," he replied, "we will test you. What is your preference? Perhaps a scene from a film you have loved?"

I was struck stupid – and dumb. What was a scene I had loved? Then it came to me – Merle Oberon's role as Cathy in the film *Wuthering Heights* with Laurence Olivier. How I loved that movie. Some films one never forgets and others become a blur. I have never forgotten one single scene in either *Wuthering Heights* or Noël Coward's *Brief Encounter*. They both remain embedded in my memory forever.

"Yes," I said, "I do have a preference, Mr. Powell. The scene from *Wuthering Heights* where Cathy tells her old nurse played by Dame Flora Robson that she is going to marry Edgar Linton, but that she will always love Heathcliff because he is her very soul and life."

Above: Hazel and football star Dennis Compton when Hazel kicked off for the team

"Good," said Mr. Powell. "I will send to Hollywood for the scene from the movie. I think I will direct the test myself. Thank you so much, Miss Court, for coming to see us."

The interview had been short, to the point, and very fruitful. I reeled out of there like a spinning top. A few weeks later, I was sent to Denham Studios for the test shoot. Michael Powell was tough and stern, but so very good and wonderfully visual. I enjoyed working with him very much. He taught me a lot in a very short time. I will always hear him saying, "Films are moving pictures. Therefore, when making them, one must capture the eyes, and the eye must remember."

The Rank contract went through, and I was set to test for *The Red Shoes*. It was the story of a ballet dancer who had to make many sacrifices, and it showed how her emotions and her way of life interfered with love. The script and the part were both terrific.

The test was arranged, and the brilliant cameraman, Jack Cardiff, photographed me. The test was very successful, and I was sent to study ballet at the Royal Ballet Company at Covent Garden. Vera Volkova, a very impressive Russian lady, was to be my teacher. I must point out that the script as it was written then was more about the inner emotions of the ballerina and included very little dancing. I worked hard at it, but I was not as good as a professional dancer.

At this same time, the Royal Ballet Company was presenting *The Three-Cornered Hat* with Robert Helpmann, Léonide Massine and the beautiful Moira Shearer. It was a truly marvellous production, and Moira Shearer took London by storm. I was at the opening night and I will never forget it.

Suddenly, things began to change. Powell and Pressburger signed Robert Helpmann to the film. I knew Moira Shearer would soon follow. The script was rewritten to include much more dance. They were right, of course. There was no question about that. The movie became a classic and a very famous musical. I was sad to lose such a great part, and to know I had come so close to playing it, but I knew that Moira was perfect for the role.

STEPHEN WARD, CLIVEDON AND THE PROFUMO SCANDAL

Halfway through the training with Vera Volkova, I sprained my ankle. The Rank Organisation sent me to have it examined by a brilliant bone doctor, and here begins another tale. The doctor's name was Stephen Ward, and he had many famous clients, Winston Churchill among them. Along with Christine Keeler and Mandy Rice Davies, Ward was to figure many years later in the Profumo scandal – a scandal that rocked England, and nearly brought down the government of the day. Much has since been written about Stephen Ward and none of it very good.

Two films were made about his life and depicted him as a bit of a spivvy character. I found none of this to be true. The man that I knew was no quack but a powerful doctor with very healing hands. He was also gracious, charming, knowledgeable, a brilliant artist – especially in black-and-white portraiture – and very good looking.

Stephen asked me out, and I went. As always, he was charming and romantic. He talked mostly about art, and I was totally captivated by him. He told me that most weekends he went down to Clivedon on the River Thames and I should go down with him sometime. Clivedon was the magnificent home of the Astors and the scene of what would later become known as the Profumo scandal.

The Daily Express broke the story, and David Frost kept pounding the scandal on the TV show, *That Was the Week That Was.* Jingles were sung about it, and fireworks exploded all over London. I did not join Stephen in Clivedon and will never know what I missed down there but, from what I heard, everyone met and had a rollicking good time. Then the scandal broke.

Here is how it all got started. John Profumo was England's Minister of Defence. He was married to an exquisite actress named Valerie Hobson who starred in many important English films. Profumo was also having an affair with a friend of Stephen Ward's named Christine Keeler. I met her once in Stephen's waiting room. She was lovely, full of fun, and had a great, very wicked laugh. Unfortunately, she was also seeing a very handsome Russian *chargé d'affaires.*

Profumo was accused of being a traitor, and Christine Keeler was accused of selling to the Russians secrets she had gotten from Profumo. Mixed up somewhere in the middle of it all was Mandy Rice Davies. (Stephen was named procurer of many beautiful women for many famous male visitors to Clivedon.)

Opposite Page: Glamour shot of Hazel

Ultimately, Profumo resigned, Christine Keeler was jailed for awhile, and I believe Mandy Rice Davies went to Israel.

I don't believe Profumo was a traitor. His wife Valerie stuck by his side and never divorced him. He went on to do marvellous humanitarian work in the East End of London. Whatever indiscretions John Profumo may have committed were long ago wiped out by the good he has subsequently done in the world.

Following the scandal, Stephen Ward was found guilty of living off the avails of prostitution and, on the last day of the trial, committed suicide by overdosing on sleeping tablets. He was let down and totally disowned by all his friends. I remember him as a man who was overloaded with talent, always kind, and very interesting. I hope Stephen's soul is healed and at peace. I am well aware that there are people who will disagree with me, but I must write about Stephen as I found him. Individuals often perceive people and events very differently. If that wasn't the case, there would be no interesting books, movies, or plays, and I would not be writing my memoirs.

RAYMOND BLACKBURN MEMORY NUMBER ONE: THE PAINTING

After I signed with the Rank Organisation, a piece appeared in the London papers about me. The story was authored by Raymond Blackburn, M.P. (Member of Parliament), who had made his maiden speech in the House of Commons, moving Winston Churchill to declare that it was "Just brilliant. One of the finest." Blackburn wrote about me in glowing colours, mentioning my red hair and green eyes, and chastising the Rank Organisation for not using me properly.

I received a telephone call from Mr. Blackburn asking me if I would join him for lunch, which I did. I found him very attractive with a brilliant mind that covered many subjects. We had a delightful luncheon. At its conclusion he asked me to have lunch with him again, saying he wanted me to meet a friend of his – a marvellous painter who would definitely enjoy painting me. I was flattered.

Lunch was arranged at The Pheasantry, the famous restaurant in Chelsea. Artists, writers, and all sorts of famous people gathered there. It was undoubtedly the "in" place of the day. I arrived not knowing whom I was going to meet. As I scanned the room, I saw to my astonishment, that Raymond Blackburn was sitting at a table with Augustus John, a famous English painter, and Pietro Annigoni, an Italian painter who had just painted the Queen of England.

I was about to run when Mr. Blackburn caught up with me. "No, you don't. You will enjoy these two people."

I sat down and shook hands with these two very famous artists, both very boisterous and larger than life. I remember thinking, "Hopefully my voice will be drowned out." The luncheon was wild and hilarious. I played tennis with my eyeballs as they told their stories, each trying to top the other. Annigoni had to leave early, which he did with appropriate larger-than-life flair.

Augustus John used the tablecloth to sketch me. Laughing and joking he said, "You need better than a white tablecloth, little redhead." Taking my hand, he said goodbye to Raymond and announced that he was going to paint me. Then he threw over his shoulder with glee, "Lunch was memorable, dear Raymond."

With great gusto, off we went to his studio in Chelsea. A very impressive room greeted me, with large windows that took over one whole wall. I was reminded of the set from the opera *La Bohème*. Even the sofa and wicker chair were there. Only, Augustus John was going to paint me, not sing to me. Work began, and I could hardly believe such a great painter was going to do a rendering of me.

I noticed he was working in pastel, crayon and charcoal, and all went well for awhile. Silence reigned supreme. I

was very relaxed on my wicker chair. Suddenly, he screamed that he could not capture my mouth. "It's there one minute and gone the next!"

"I'm sorry," I said, rather meekly.

"It needs to be made love to," he announced, arms flying in the air.

"Oh, no it doesn't," I declared. "It's perfectly happy the way it is."

With that, he stormed out of the studio. I jumped down and started to look at his wonderfully inspired work piled high on benches. The gypsy scenes were hypnotic, full of romance, colour and energy. I was overwhelmed and could have stayed there gazing forever.

Mr. John returned with a large loaf of white bread, which he then began to rub on the drawing – on my mouth? Working for another hour, he finally said, "That's it. There is the mouth." He lifted the work down from the easel and asked, "Would you like to see it?"

The picture was tremendous. The concentration was on my eyes, not my mouth, and it had a feeling of illusion about it. I still wonder what became of the picture. A gallery owner once told me he thought he saw it sold at Sotheby's for one hundred thousand pounds.

Augustus John was a very impressive man, probably six feet four inches tall, with a head of magnificent snow white hair and a long white beard. He was very handsome and must have been in his middle eighties at the time.

We parted with a big hug. He tugged my hair and said, "I captured this, didn't I?" He certainly did. My hair was half the picture. It was the experience of a lifetime.

RAYMOND BLACKBURN MEMORY NUMBER TWO: CHARTWELL

Another Raymond Blackburn memory involves the time he invited me to a luncheon at the home of Mary Churchill, a very impressive lady who had the gift of making everyone feel welcome and at ease. Mary lived next door to Chartwell, the home of her father, Winston Churchill.

We had a splendid lunch and then we went for a swim in the pool designed and built by Winston Churchill. There was a gorgeous waterfall cascading from an upper level down into the pool. I swam, and enjoyed every moment with a secret smile on my face, just knowing whose pool it was.

Afterwards, Raymond suggested we dress and wander over to the goldfish pond on the grounds of Chartwell. "It's always possible," he said, "that he might be there talking to the goldfish." He *was* there, sitting under the

Left: Glamour shot of Hazel

125G-P112

Various Glamour shots of Hazel

bamboo arbour, doing just that – talking to the goldfish. From where we were, it sounded like one was named George. I spoke quietly to Raymond, telling him that I did not plan to intrude on the reverie of Churchill, who looked so peaceful, at one with his fish. Sporting a straw hat with a wide brim and a loose beige jacket, he looked like a Monet painting.

Raymond said, "Come on, I know him." I didn't move, hidden behind the trees. More than meeting this great man of the 20th century, I just loved looking at him communing in nature, at such peace. Many have spoken to him, but how many have watched him talking to his fish? It was a rare and unforgettable picture.

LAST AND FINAL MEMORY OF RAYMOND BLACKBURN

Raymond Blackburn informed me that I was invited to a small dinner party given by Lady Emerald Cunard of Cunard Shipping Lines. The party was to be held at her splendid apartment in the Dorchester Hotel and we were to wear dinner dress.

Dinner with Lady Emerald Cunard was a marvellous experience. She was petite and perfect in every way – beautifully gowned and with a sparkle to her personality that was almost naughty. She wore the fabulous Cunard Emeralds. From the necklace to the earrings and bracelet, they were the largest emeralds I have ever seen.

Among the guests were former Prime Minister Anthony Eden and Oliver Messel, world-renowned stage, screen, and costume designer. The conversation was fascinating and sometimes over my head.

Raymond Blackburn suddenly said, "You are very quiet tonight, Hazel."

Lady Cunard piped up, saying that I was very pretty and didn't need to talk. "Come with me, my dear, and I will show you all of my art," she said, gently taking my arm. Lady Cunard was very expressive as she showed me her impressive art collection, and generous with her pearls of wisdom. Two things she said have always stayed with me. First, she told me that if you possess good art, you always paint your walls off-white. Secondly, she instructed me to always sleep a weekend in my guest room to make sure it is comfortable and enjoyable. I have always had off-white walls and have made it a point to sleep in my guest rooms.

Raymond Blackburn was the catalyst for so many rich experiences that I now treasure as memories. He slipped out of my life quietly, unlike the way he entered. In his wake, he left a colourful tapestry of enduring moments with artists, paintings, goldfish, and ladies in emeralds.

LONDON AFTER THE WAR

After the War, London was swinging. The city never seemed to sleep. I know I certainly didn't. We worked all day and then, at night, we changed into beautiful ball gowns and long white gloves. Can you imagine wearing white gloves today? Only the Queen still does.

Whenever we were to attend an opening night in London, we would have to dress beautifully. If we were working, the studios would let us off early to get our hair washed and styled and get into our exquisite gowns. Those days were true, pure glamour.

Gorgeous limos would carry us from our respective studios into London to attend a film premiere or the opening of a play. Then we would end up at Les Ambassadors – or "Les A" as we called it – for dinner. Then on to the Milroy Nightclub for dancing 'til dawn.

Everybody who was anybody could be found at those two places. One day at Les A while I was having lunch, a whisper went round the room that Ingrid Bergman was coming in. As she appeared, the whole restaurant went silent – and then we all stood and applauded. She was absolutely luminous, and she made the whole room glow, electrifying us all. Some actresses have that quality, like Sophia Loren. Vivien Leigh had it too, only with a bit of a difference – she was more like a glowing cat.

Those were glamorous, wonderful times. From *Annie Get Your Gun* to *Oklahoma* and *South Pacific*, American musicals flocked to the London stage. As the Cockneys say, those musicals hit us with a wallop, and they healed the wounds of war. We loved them all.

Danny Kaye came to the London Palladium for the first time and was a tremendous success. I was at the opening night, which lasted until 2.00 a.m., when he was carried through the streets of London, shoulder high, with all of us singing his songs and hailing him as a great artist. My sister was his press representative, and she said that working for him was one of the highlights of her life. He was funny – and moody, but one forgave that.

DERMOT WALSH AND RANDOM HARVEST

In 1947, a handsome Irish actor named Dermot Walsh made a big hit in a film starring Margaret Lockwood. It was called *Hungry Hill*, from a book written by Daphne Du Maurier. Though I am credited with a small role in that film, I was not actually in the movie. The film did play a role in our meeting, however, because it was while Dermot was doing publicity for the film – and I was doing publicity for other pictures – that we met.

It was because Dermot and I were both under contract with the Rank Organisation that they sent us to Brussels together – and what started as a publicity trip quickly turned into a romantic expedition. This started our love affair. First, we toured Britain in the stage play of James Hilton's *Random Harvest*, adapted by Moie Charles and Barbara Toye. It had been a major motion picture with Greer Garson and Ronald Colman. We found our roles so rewarding that we put together a company and took the play to Germany to play to American and British soldiers. First stop, Hamburg, where an interesting moment in my life presented itself.

We had finished rehearsing for opening night when the manager asked me if I would like to see the rest of the Hamburg Opera House. We walked along the corridors, viewing the stage from a number of areas.

Then he said, "Let's make history."

Coming upon a lovely silk padded door along the corridor of the first tier, he took from his coat pocket a large key.

"Please enter," he said, inserting the key into the door.

I did just that, and stepped into a lovely theatre box.

"You are the first to enter this box," he then informed me, "since Adolf Hitler left it."

For a few moments, I couldn't move. I was amazed. There was a very musty smell in the air, and a very strange, creepy feeling came over me. I thanked him for making me a part of history, and then hurried to my dressing room – and to a deep think.

Below: Programme for Random Harvest (1942)

Random Harvest, the story of a soldier who loses his memory in the war, was a big success. In the story, the soldier returns from the war and doesn't realise his secretary is actually his wife – until the very end of the play, as he recovers his memory. It is very touching. I played the role of Smithy, the wife, and it was very eerie – a really weird feeling. I experienced exactly what it would be like if my husband lost his memory.

We were playing at an Air Force base outside of Berlin, and thanks to the fact that the Berlin airlift was in progress, whispered lines quickly became a shouting match. The last line of the play, where the soldier's memory is restored and he turns round and says, "Smithy, you… you all the time," and I say, "Yes, yes, me all the time," became almost funny, because we were playing in a tin hut and couldn't really whisper. We had to yell across the stage. I can still hear the roar of the planes. Strange memories.

Above Left: Hazel and father G. W. Court on her wedding day to Dermot Walsh

Above Right: Surrounded by fans, Dermot carries new bride Hazel over the threshold at the wedding reception locale

The company toured most cities in Germany. We saw the entire town of Kassell reduced to a great mountain of bricks. Nothing was left standing. We could not believe our eyes. Hanover had also been bombed to rubble, and we got lost there at night, which was really spooky. The German driver said he recognised no streets. After driving round for hours, we met some American soldiers who took us back to our hostel.

In Minden, we were staying in a country house which had been converted for us into a small hostel. Being very tired, I went to bed and lay down immediately. Suddenly, my chest felt like a heavy weight was sitting on it, and I became very short of breath. Every time I lay down, this pressure was on my chest. The whole room was closing in on me, and I realised I was incapable of lying there a moment longer. I managed to get to Dermot's room which was next door. He calmed me down, saying, "I will take your room."

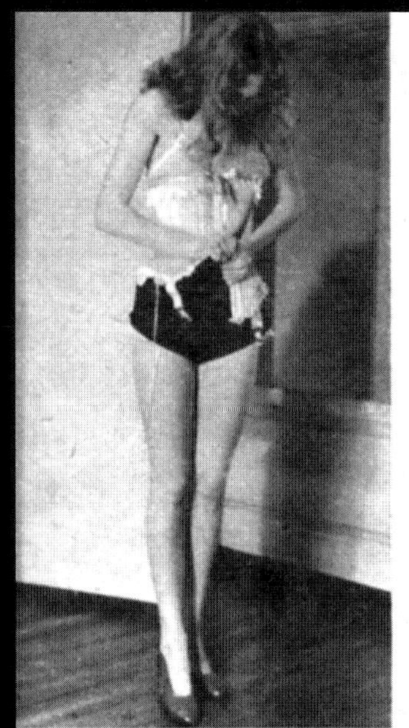

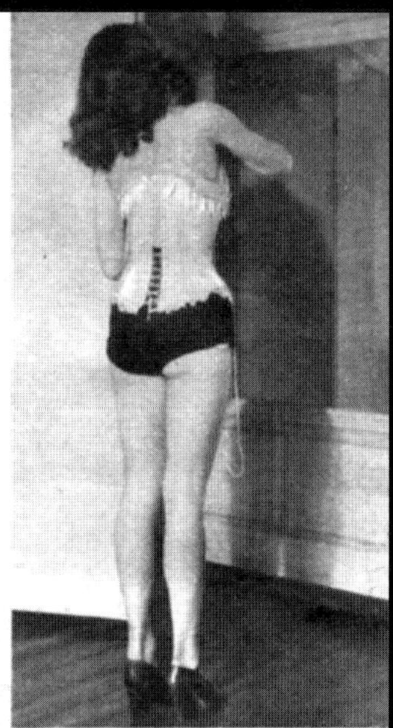

Life Was Very Complicated . . .   . . . In the Good Old Days
Hazel luckily has a wasp waist, but old-style corsets are needed to give the curves fashionable in the 'nineties.

Miss 1946 Steps into 1896

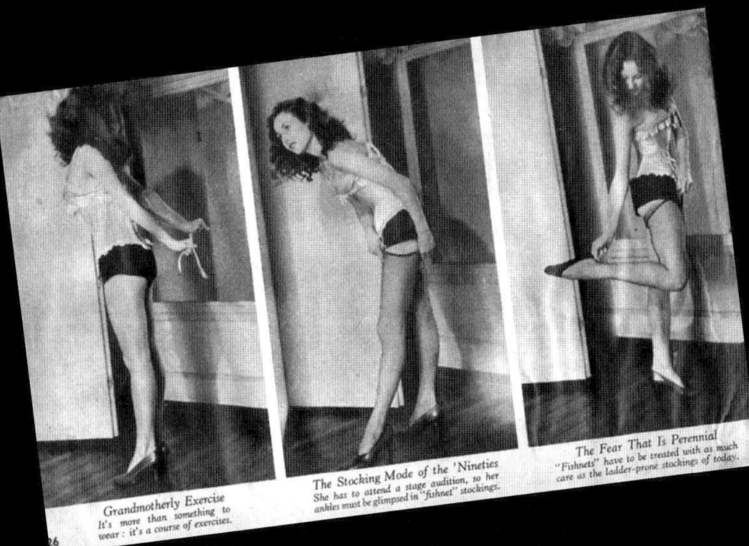

Grandmotherly Exercise
It's more than something to wear : it's a course of exercises.

The Stocking Mode of the 'Nineties
She has to attend a stage audition, so her ankles must be glimpsed in "fishnet" stockings.

The Fear That Is Perennial
"Fishnets" have to be treated with as much care as the ladder-prone stockings of today.

26

Various Glamour shots of Hazel

Not fifteen minutes later, he was knocking at my door, saying, "The bar is still open. Let's go down and have a drink."

The bar man said we looked very pale. We told him of our experience, and he told us, "Well, if you look behind the wardrobe, you will see a sealed up archway. It once led to a turret where seven Jews were walled up and died." No one said another word. We spent the night sleeping in the lobby.

Düsseldorf was our last stop. We played to rows and rows of soldiers in full dress uniforms. There were generals and other officers, and I felt very proud to be there, and to be able to help break up the tension from the War. It was all very worthwhile and made for great memories.

In 1949, we would marry, and Dermot Walsh would become my first husband.

MARY, QUEEN OF SCOTS

We were in Edinburgh, Scotland, acting in *Random Harvest*, and we were backstage on opening night. We were told that the Duke of Hamilton, who lived at Holyrood Palace in Edinburgh, was in the audience. It always lent an energetic flair to the production when we knew "someone" was in the audience.

Nine o'clock the next morning, the phone rang, and to my amazement, it was the Duke of Hamilton.

"Good morning, Miss Court," the Duke began, "I loved your performance last night. It was a wonderful play. Anyway, I have just read in the newspaper that you have always wanted to play the role of Mary, Queen of Scots. I wondered if you would like to come to the palace and have a look at the real death mask of Mary."

My voice was nowhere to be found. I was stunned. Eventually, the words came, and I thanked him profusely, saying that it would be a tremendous moment in my life.

"Wonderful," he replied, "I will send a car round for you at 9:30 tomorrow morning."

With a bump, I sat down. To see the face of Mary, Queen of Scots was beyond my wildest dreams. It was one of those times in one's life when everything seems to be going right. I fairly floated through the next twenty-four hours.

The car arrived as prescribed and, a little bit past 9.30 a.m., I was at the palace. Holyrood is so steeped in history and mystery that a formidable, strange feeling entered my body as I entered the palace. History lingers in the air. I was taken into the Duke's study. He was a charming man. We had coffee and talked about Mary.

At the end of the room, there was an enormous vault. Mary's death mask was kept in the vault, along with a beautiful lock of her red hair, the famous casket of letters, and the lace puff she was wearing round her neck when she walked to her execution. The death mask was very carefully brought out and laid on the table in front of me. There was a faint smile on her lips... peace, at last, perhaps. The look on her lovely face was beyond anything I could put into words. Unexpectedly, tears came into my eyes. To die by the sword of an executioner was very wrong.

As I gazed at this mystical mask, I found myself fascinated with her nose. All the paintings I had seen have given her a rather large and long nose, which was totally inaccurate. She had a chiselled, very beautiful nose, and nostrils that looked as if they had been carved out of ivory. I have never seen anything as arresting, and I was awestruck – riveted by this historical face.

The Duke of Hamilton returned her to the vault, saying "There are a number of supposed death masks, but I assure you, this is the original."

We shook hands and I thanked him for allowing me the privilege of this private viewing. They were pieces of history. In a total daze, I left the palace.

Dermot Walsh and I had an old cottage in Kent, on the trail of the Canterbury monks. Across the lane in an old manor house lived the Count and Countess del Abedoy'ere. We had bought the cottage from a relation of the Count. They had a very interesting daughter named Sybil who reminded me of a character from a Brontë story. At the age of eighteen years old, she had published her first book, called *The Passionate Shepherd*, which was quite successful but is probably long since out of print.

I was standing at the open living room window of our cottage when, in the distance, came Sybil, with flowing hair, large country boots and a colourful peasant shirt half hidden by an oversized sweater.

"Hello, you're back," she called.

As she came nearer, I found myself mesmerised by her nose. "Forgive me for staring at you," I explained, "but I've just seen your nose in Holyrood Palace on the death mask of Mary, Queen of Scots. I'm in shock." I was rooted to the spot. With those wonderful flaring nostrils, her nose was the same.

She laughed. "But, of course. I am a direct descendant of Mary on the French side – the de Guise family. My mother has the bedcover embroidered by the ladies in waiting to Mary, Queen of Scots – the Four Marys."

Above: Engraving of Mary, Queen of Scots given to Hazel by the Count and Countess del Abedoy'ere

Opposite Page:

Top: Publicity still for Meet Me at Dawn (1947)

Bottom: Poster for Meet Me at Dawn (1947)

Above Top: Publicity still for Meet Me at Dawn (1947)

Above Bottom: Sketch for Hazel's costume for the same film

Another member of Sybil's family ended up giving me an engraving of the famous Queen of Scots, which I keep on my desk.

It must have been thirty years later that I was driving in to stay in Cornwall at the Boscundle Manor Hotel. As I drove in, I remember seeing a lady on the steps of the hotel, singing "Anyone here? Anyone own this hotel? Any rooms for one night? Anyone home?" I laughed to myself, because it was in such a typical English manner that the woman was calling out.

Later that evening, I was quietly eating my dinner when the owner came over to me. She said, "There is someone here that would like to meet you. It is the Countess del Abedoy'ere." It was not the Countess I had known – which is why I did not recognise her standing on the steps. The Countess I had known had died and the Count had married again. This lady, Charlotte del Abedoy'ere was a wonderful, larger than life character. As for Sybil, she had not pursued her writing talent, but married and had a family.

MEET ME AT DAWN

In 1947, on *Meet Me At Dawn* I was billed as "Introducing Hazel Court for 20th Century Fox." It was a period film taken from a French story called "The Duellist." It is about a young man making his living in the year 1900 by fighting duels on behalf of other parties. He is hired to injure a leading politician and gets romantically involved with the politician's daughter. They are at a fair, and she twists her ankle. He rescues her, and takes her back to his apartment. That is where their love affair begins.

This film starred Stanley Holloway in the role of the duellist's sidekick, and he was sheer charm. It also starred Margaret Rutherford and William Eythe, an American star who made his name in *The Song of Bernadette* with Jennifer Jones. For me, it was a good part and my first starring role.

I tested for the part and after the showing of the test, to which I was invited, I was asked to step outside by the producer, Marcel Hellman. He told me they wanted to "discuss business" – the business was me. After about thirty minutes, I was told I had got the part.

Along with Peter Creswell, Thornton Freeland – a charming, comfortable gentleman – directed the film. Stanley Holloway made us laugh a lot, as did Margaret Rutherford, and we all had fun. On one occasion, she informed us she had a stomach disorder and therefore a lot of wind – or in American slang, gas.

"I can't help it," she informed us very seriously. "You all must learn to live with it." She was a great actress and one very funny lady. I remember numerous sandwiches she consumed which were never ordered but just seemed to appear out of nowhere – cucumber, egg and salmon. Mugs and mugs of tea washed them down. Yes, I remember Margaret very well.

Meet Me at Dawn was well reviewed and very successful for me. Looking back, I remember how relaxed we all were. The acting was a joy. I don't think we had the pressure then that we have these days. It was such a delicate film – and you could say it had a thin story line. Yet it was charming and entertaining. That story could never be sold today. Times have changed.

HOLIDAY CAMP

Director Ken Annakin's first feature, *Holiday Camp* (1947), was my next film. He had made wonderful documentaries but decided *Holiday Camp* was the right choice for his debut into features. He was right. It was an enormous success. The film was loaded with stars – Jack Warner, Kathleen Harrison, Dame Flora Robson, Jimmy Hanley, Dennis Price, Esma Cannon, Yvonne Owen, Diana Dors and me as one of the Huggetts.

It was the story of the Huggett family who went away for a holiday at the third Butlin's Holiday Camp at Filey on the Yorkshire Coast. Such holiday camps first opened by Billy Butlin (later to be named Sir) in 1936 following his success in the development of amusement parks. They were a major breakthrough.

After the war, the Butlin's camps became a favourite of families who looked forward to entertainment and activities the whole family could enjoy for about a week's pay. There, all social classes

JUNE—IN JANUARY

Everywhere in Britain yesterday it was cold, wet, wintry — everywhere but at Shepherd's Bush, where a sunny bathing-pool in the studios took the actors' minds off grim reality. The occasion was Sydney Box's new film, "Holiday Camp," and the story said that Hazel Court had to win a beauty prize presented by Patricia Roc, sitting on the left. The script-writers had an easy time. Look at Hazel and see how easy it was to make the story come true.

Right: Diana Dors and Hazel in a publicity shot
Holiday Camp (1947)

Above Top: Poster for Holiday Camp (1947)

Above Bottom: Cutting featuring Hazel

mixed together, breaking all sorts of barriers. We generally played together, danced together and sat down to meals together. Ken was a magnificent director and used his documentary background to film the real camp at the peak of the season.

Above and Below: Two publicity shots from Holiday Camp (1947)

Another breakthrough on this film was the fact that my character had a baby and was unmarried. In the movie, the father never turned up and no one ever spoke about him. The real life son of Jimmy Hanley and Dinah Sheridan played the baby, and he was the bonniest baby you ever saw; he grew up to have a wonderful career in British politics, becoming a minister in John Major's government. He had all the fun and great sense of humour of his father, plus the charm of his lovely mother, Dinah Sheridan (remember *Genevieve*?).

In the film, I fall in love with Jimmy Hanley. In real life, we became great friends, and I was saddened when he died so young – long before his time. He was only fifty-one, and died of cancer.

In the story, I was crowned "The Holiday Princess" in a competition at the swimming pool. After the film was released, every year in every Butlin's Camp there was a "Holiday Princess." Words can't describe what a magnificent time we all had making the film – so much laughter! We were recovering from the War, and life was to be enjoyed. We were alive. For an excellent and entertaining story of the making of this great film, see Ken Annakin's autobiography, *So You Wanna Be a Director?,* published by Tomahawk Press.

After *Holiday Camp*, Ken Annakin went on to make many great films which are considered classics today, including *Miranda* with the delectable Glynis Johns, *Quartet* (by Somerset Maugham), *Battle of the*

Above: Publicity shots from Holiday Camp (1947)

Bulge, and everybody's favourite, *Those Magnificent Men in Their Flying Machines*.

I met Ken again nearly thirty years later in California. My husband and I were dining at a restaurant in Santa Monica, California when a hand tapped me on a shoulder, and a voice said, "I know you." Ken was with his lovely, mischievous wife, Pauline. We picked right up where we left off all those years ago and have since become very close friends.

In recent years, the Butlin's Holiday Camp where we filmed was demolished. All that is left is a pile of rubble. What a pity. It was part of history. If you visit the site and listen carefully, you might still hear the strains of "Knees Up Mother Brown," echoing as the North Sea breeze blows across the camp ruins.

DANCING WITH THE WOUNDED SOLDIERS

Along came the days of The Jitterbug, Frank Sinatra driving the bobby-soxers mad with his great crooning, and the name Joe Louis – world heavyweight champion boxer. Everywhere I went, I heard his name. The 1948 Olympic Games came to London, and I was at those magical games to see Emil Zatopek of Czechoslovakia win the 10,000 metres. Picasso was in exile in Paris, swearing never to return to his native Spain while Franco ruled there. In 1949, the new look by Christian Dior was making all the magazine covers. I loved it – the long, full skirts with masses of lace underneath.

On Saturday nights, I would go down to a hospital at East Grinstead to dance with unfortunate soldiers, sailors, and airmen who had lost their arms, their legs, or their faces, or been badly burnt in the War. The famous plastic surgeon Sir Archibald McIndoe had erected the hospital for plastic surgery and recuperation. We would go down to the hospital dressed in exquisite gowns and make ourselves look glamorous. The first time on the dance floor, I nearly passed out as the soldier I danced with had no hands and very little face. I recovered and held him, and many more to follow, very tight. As I write about that chapter in my life, I still see and feel their faces, those soldiers who gave so much to us all. I remember those times with love and sorrow.

McIndoe was probably among the first plastic surgeons of his kind. He would make eyelids where there were none, and a nose where one used to be. He married Connie King, the wife of the late George King, producer and director of my second film, *Gaiety George*. McIndoe is one of my heroes and one person I am pleased and proud to have known.

Above: Christmas card from the Hanley family to hazel (Actor Jimmy Hanley and wife, actress Dinah Sheridan

Towards the end of the 1940s, after all the horrors we had been through, after the bombings and the air raid shelters and being uptight every night of our lives, a lovely thing happened in London. Suddenly this gorgeous, world-famous ballerina named Margot Fonteyn danced across the stage of Covent Garden Theatre. Covent Garden was sold out. Fonteyn was a brilliant dancer and a delight to behold. Opening nights were magical, and the beauty, grace and talent she had brought to us were in stark contrast to what we had lived through in the War.

The London audiences were great, as always. They always applaud and scream and yell, as they did then – and it felt like a totally new beginning. We were finally getting back to talent and beautiful things. Far away from Covent Garden and the adulation of the world, Fonteyn died in Panama, after caring for her Panamanian husband who had become paralysed and wheelchair-bound following a shooting. Her star still glitters.

A CUP OF TEA AND A CURRANT BUN

During my twenties, I posed in many photographic sessions for Baron, the world-renowned royal court photographer to Queen Elizabeth II.

One day while working with Baron on a special magazine cover shot, I noticed a very attractive young man moving giant lamps and setting up shots. It was obvious he knew a great deal about photography.

"Hazel," Baron suddenly said, "would you like a cup of tea?"

"Oh, yes," I replied, always ready.

Baron shouted across the room to the attractive young man, "Tony, get Hazel a cup of tea! Oh, and a currant bun."

"Yes, Sir Baron," Tony replied, being cheeky.

This Page: One of several portraits by Baron, Royal Court photographer

Opposite Page:

Top: Baby Sally Walsh, Hazel and Walsh family

Bottom: Hazel and Sally Walsh

Baron looked at me and said, "I apologise. I forgot to introduce you. That was Anthony Armstrong Jones. He's a bloody good photographer, probably better than me in the end. And of course, he's also dating Princess Margaret."

My mouth dropped open. The hot steaming cup of tea and a currant bun came gliding through the door, served to me by the very man we'd all been hearing about in the paper. There he was lifting the lights and setting up shots, and behaving as if he were just a photographer's assistant – and a waiter!

Tony Armstrong Jones did marry Princess Margaret, and he became Lord Snowdon. His photographic work is truly marvellous. It is very expansive and entirely different from the work of the wonderful Baron.

So history travels on. A cup of tea and a currant bun made my day – and of course being waited upon by the future Lord Snowdon.

SALLY IS BORN

My daughter Sally was born on the 7th May 1950. She was beautiful and bonny, a black-haired gal, with the Irish of her father Dermot. She weighed eight-and-a-half pounds. The strain of the birth was almost too much for me, but I heard the doctor say, "Oh, dear, I have never lost a patient yet", and I did survive.

Sally would grow up to have big eyes like her mother, along with talents in painting and writing. She has become a specialist in animation art, particularly the antique pieces. I am very proud of her, and she has taught me a lot. I hope she has gathered a little of the world from me, as I have lived a long time.

Dermot and I, along with baby Sally, lived in Kent. Our village was called Cowden and our cottage was on the trail of the Canterbury Tales. We had five acres of apple trees. It was an idyllic life and far removed from the stage and film world. Nevertheless, the film world kept me busy.

I made many films during that period, and I greatly enjoyed all of them. Two of those films I made with my husband, Dermot Walsh – *Ghost Ship* (1952) and *Counterspy* (1953), both for director Vernon Sewell. The 1959 film, The *Wreck of the Mary Deare* borrowed a lot from *Ghost Ship*.

DEVIL GIRL FROM MARS

In 1954, I made a film called *Devil Girl from Mars* which was an enormous success considering that it was a low budget film. I'm told it plays somewhere in the world every day.

In addition to myself, it starred Patricia Laffan, Hugh McDermott, Adrienne Corri, John Laurie and Joseph Tomelty. This goofy, but fun, sci-fi opus has gained a cult following in the U.S. It is described as a true gem of Atomic Age entertainment.

About the film, *TV Guide* says, "This inferior British retread of *The Day the Earth Stood Still* takes place at a small Scottish Inn where a stereotypical barmaid (Corri), reporter (McDermott), disillusioned model (yours truly), scientist (Tomelty) and escaped murderer (Peter Reynolds) are visited by a sexy, leather-clad female Martian (Laffan) accompanied by her silly-looking robot. She announces to the shocked bar patrons that Mars has just had a revolution and women have taken over. She says that she has come to earth to kidnap healthy men to take back to Mars for breeding purposes. The men refuse, but Reynolds (the murderer) goes with Laffan in her spaceship and manages to blow it up, sacrificing his life so that poor Earthmen won't have to breed with leather-clad Martian women."

When we were making the film, even though it featured well-known stars and theatre people, we thought, "What are we doing? It will never see the light of day." It was truly ahead of its time. Even though it seemed preposterous to us that it would be a big hit, that genre had not yet become popular, so we had done something groundbreaking and revolutionary.

I laugh when I think about it, but I still get fan mail, and I'm even told Steven Spielberg got some ideas from it. Nearly fifty years later, I wonder if women in leather still rule Mars.

THE CURSE OF FRANKENSTEIN

In 1957 I was excited to be asked to star with Peter Cushing in *The Curse of Frankenstein*. I loved every moment of making the film.

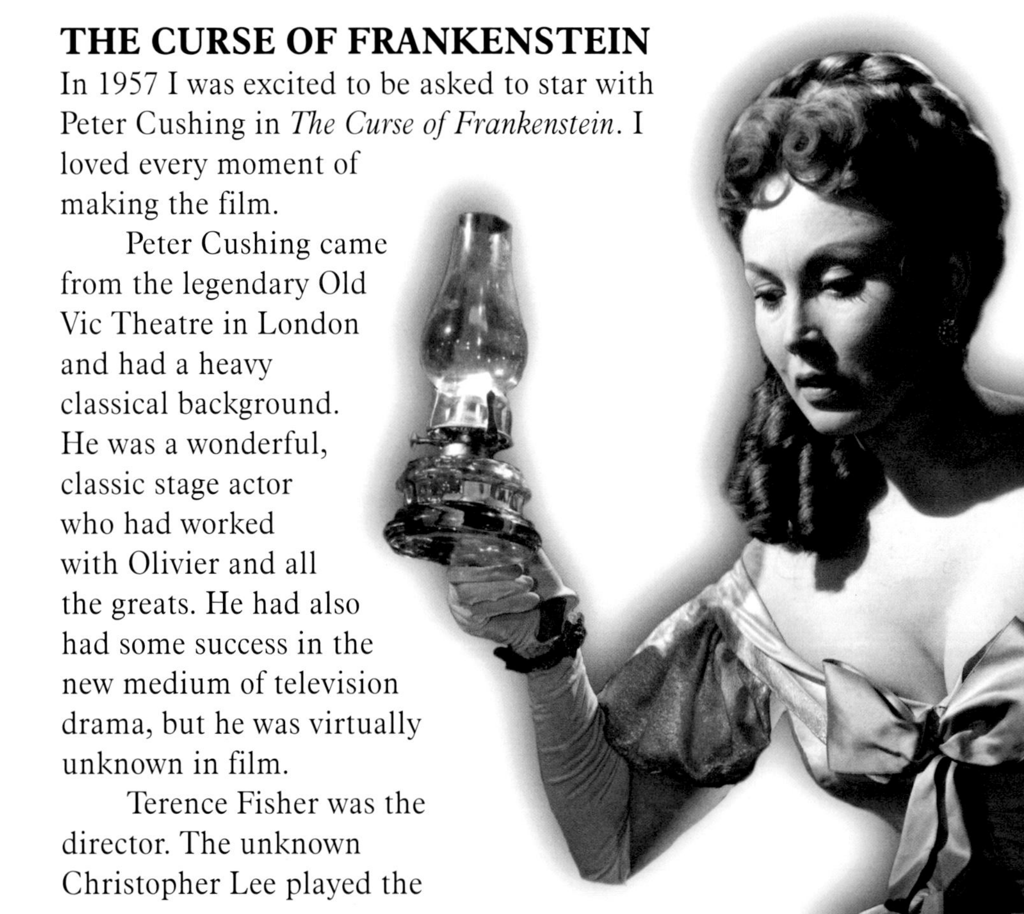

Peter Cushing came from the legendary Old Vic Theatre in London and had a heavy classical background. He was a wonderful, classic stage actor who had worked with Olivier and all the greats. He had also had some success in the new medium of television drama, but he was virtually unknown in film.

Terence Fisher was the director. The unknown Christopher Lee played the

This Page: Rank glamour shots

Next two Pages: Various magazine covers

HOME REVIEW 6d
POPULAR HOME JOURNAL
No. 251. (Estab. 1926) FEBRUARY, 1947 MONTHLY
HAZEL COURT (See page 30)

True Romances
JUNE 1946
1/-
HAZEL COURT
TV mirror and DISC NEWS
EVERY WEDNESDAY 6d
Hazel Court . . .
Do pin-ups pay? (page 16)

Picture Show
TUESDAY
FORTNIGHTLY
THREEPENCE
HAZEL COURT
& DERMOT WALSH
"MY SISTER AND I"

LEADER
MAGAZINE
44
PAGES
Photographer of Beauty
6d
27 AUGUST 1949

Week ending June 1 1957
EVERY THURSDAY
4½D
Picturegoer
THE NATIONAL FILM AND
ENTERTAINMENT WEEKLY
HOLLYWOOD
MEN AND
THEIR MORALS
–startling
new
investigation
HAZEL
COURT

True Romances
October 1944
1/-
WEEK ENDING APRIL 26 1952
EVERY WEDNESDAY
ILLUSTRATED
At Home With
The Stars
Pages 28–29
FOOTWEAR WEIRD AND WONDERFUL
THE WEEKLY
TELEGRAPH
A KEMSLEY PUBLICATION
3D.
HAZEL COURT

Opposite Page: Hazel and Pernell Roberts in Bonanza – "The Last Trophy" (1960)

This Page:
Top Left: The Man Who Could Cheat Death (1959) – Taken from the scene in the European version of the film

Bottom Left: Vincent and Hazel in Masque of the Red Death (1964)

Above: A pin-up shot

Opposite Page: The Premature Burial (1962)

This Page: Above: Masque of the Red Death (1964)

Right: Court and Cushing in the “Pass the marmalade” scene from The Curse of Frankenstein (1957)

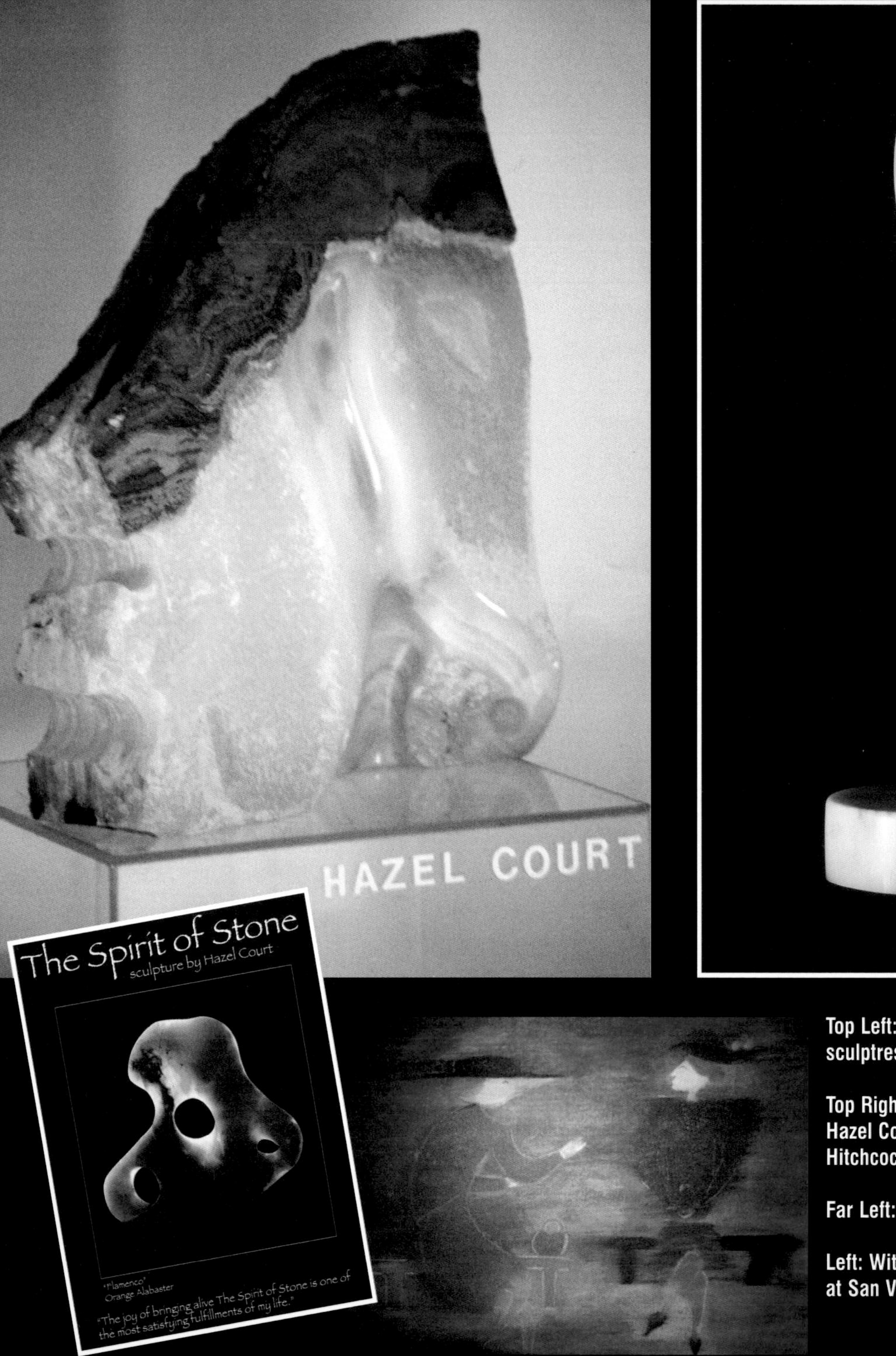

Top Left: "A Horse for the Ages" by Hazel Court, sculptress

Top Right: White marble sculpture, "Sailing" by Hazel Court, Sculptress (Owned by Alfred Hitchcock's daughter, Pat)

Far Left: From a Hazel Court sculpture brochure

Left: With the Gossips – When seen by Vincent Price at San Vicente, Hazel's career as an artist took off.

Opposite Page: Publicity Shot for The Curse of Frankenstein (1957)

Left: Director Fisher, Court and Cushing on the set of The Curse of Frankenstein (1957)

monster, Peter Cushing was Baron Frankenstein, and Robert Urquhart was the love interest and assistant to Frankenstein.

My previous starring roles and my high profile in the entertainment press was, I suppose, what attracted the producers to me. They needed one or two established names in order to increase the marketability of this film from the small Hammer Films production company. Years of Hammer horror pictures started with this film. It is widely believed that Hammer Films were responsible for many of the best horror films of the 1950s, '60s and '70s.

Little did I know how horror films would change my life.

My first meeting with Peter was in his dressing room during a lunch break at the start of the film. He was doing embroidery – cross-stitch to be exact. He was making seat covers for his dining room chairs. He was so gentle in his stitching technique, the way the needle went in and he pulled out this beautiful string. I was dumbfounded as we talked above the cross-stitch. He was so dear.

"Ah, my dear," he said, "how lovely to meet you."

He was charming and well-mannered with an impish sense of humour. As I got to know Peter better, I realised how many things he loved in the

Above Left and Right: Hazel and Lee in full makeup in the canteen at Bray during The Curse of Frankenstein (1957)

world. He loved painting, and painted a lot of watercolour flowers. He was a wonderful artist. He also loved to write, and he loved birds, animals, flowers, children, children's toys, music and his home in Whitstable. Above all, he loved his divine wife, Helen. She was his sunrise and his sunset. When she died, he wished to follow her.

Having had two great loves in my life, I do not understand the world today where people are with someone for two weeks and then they drop them. It is so wonderful to be in love and be romantic. I loved both of my husbands, God rest their souls.

Peter was a wonderful human being. I have been asked so many times by reporters, "There must be something bad somewhere, Miss Court," but there was nothing. He cared for all his fellow actors. I never heard him being bitchy about anyone. The people of the village of Whitstable were all his friends. Peter died in August of 1994, and thinking back on Peter's life, one is filled with great warmth and can imagine a golden glow the moment Peter and Helen were reunited in Heaven.

Christopher Lee's part was very physical, and he even had to lift me up and carry me like a rag doll. He and I did not have many scenes together, but we got together for lunch – which, because of his makeup, he drank through a straw, dribbling down his front. I remember him as an excellent storyteller who could go on for hours without being boring. He was always great fun, very funny, and really not scary at all. It was a delight to listen to these stories coming out of him while he was in his monster makeup.

Above Left: Hazel feeds Lee through his makeup during the making of The Curse of Frankenstein (1957)

Above Right: Hazel, Sally Walsh and a Hammer executive, The Curse of Frankenstein (1957)

He was a wonderful monster because he kind of breaks your heart. He gives the monster such a quality of gentleness that no one did in the remakes. He went on to make many, many films.

Robert Urquhart, who played the part of Frankenstein's assistant, was a very nice human being, very pleasant to work with, and quite attractive.

Sally Walsh, my young daughter, played my character Elizabeth as a child. She looked adorable, but I don't think she liked it much. She enjoyed dressing up, but was frightened of The Creature. She cried when she saw me in the crinoline – all that fabric looked like a big cage.

Working on the River Thames at Bray was such a joy; it was a unique atmosphere and we were one big family. Food plays a large part in my memory of the old studio days – bacon butties (bacon sandwiches with fried eggs inside) during makeup, fried potato cakes at the mid-morning break, fighting for large helpings of bread-and-butter pudding for lunch. We didn't think about weight. We just stayed slim. There was a roundness or voluptuousness to our thinness back then. Like Dorothy Lamour or Jayne Mansfield, women had rounded figures.

It was a very relaxed set but when the director, Terry Fisher, said action, we were all very professional. I remember a terrible thunderstorm. The floor was soaking wet on our stage, and looking up, I saw a giant hole in the roof. I ran to the producer, Anthony Hinds, yelling, "The roof is leaking! The roof is leaking!" Mr. Hinds yelled back that the rain would stop and the floor would dry. That was the way we made our films.

OUR COVER GIRL

Shines Among the Ghouls

HAZEL COURT, the beauty among the beasts in "The Curse Of Frankenstein," is making other glamour girls turn green—with envy. Hers will be the most widely screened British face in America this year.

Apart from starring in this deep-freeze chiller—tipped to be shown in more U.S. cinemas than any British film ever—she gets her own TV series for peak-night viewing on the mammoth C.B.C. TV network.

It's called "Dick And The Duchess," a weekly caper about a Yank in blue-blood England.

Not bad going for the girl whom British studios forgot. As a dewy teen-ager she was proclaimed a star by the Rank Organization. But the fanfare cracked. Soon she was in "B" films.

Now her "X" picture comeback is shaking up British show business. American producer Sheldon Reynolds has stepped in smartly and signed her to a two-year contract to make pictures here and in Hollywood.

It's enough to make our current starlets eat their own publicity. When she made "Frankenstein," friends sympathized: "No one will notice a girl among the ghouls." How wrong can they get?

SHOW PAGE

THEY'VE HOTTED THE OLD MONSTER BUT IT'S—

Such a dignified dose of horror...

BRITAIN'S first horror film in colour. . . .

So runs the proud proclamation about THE CURSE OF FRANKENSTEIN (Warner, "X" certificate) ★★.

Well, everything must have a beginning.

And not even the most pernickety critic will deny that this British prentice effort makes up for lost time.

The amount of blood, grisliness and head-hacking packed into 82 minutes—all in glorious Eastman colour—makes Shakespeare's *Titus Andronicus*, hitherto the record-holder, seem positively anæmic by dead-weight comparison.

Mary Shelley's original classic was not exactly for the squeamish; the new screen version hots up Mrs. Shelley.

By HAROLD CONWAY

The half-crazed Baron Frankenstein (PETER CUSHING) locks himself up in his Swiss castle laboratory.

From his work-bench—looking a cross between a Heath Robinson contraption and an aquarium filled with sarsaparilla—he creates a human monster.

Headless

Ingredients: The body of a dead highwayman, cut down from a gibbet (head surplus to requirements, so sawn off and dissolved in an acid bath);

The hands of a deceased sculptor, knocked off from a museum:

The brain of a famous scientist.

Baron Frankenstein pushes him over the banisters after a good dinner, coffee and liqueur.

As for the liver and lights, the Baron—armed with a little black bag—goes shopping at the local charnel-house. . . .

Not unreasonably, the resulting creature is a hideously scarred and deformed apparition — who half-strangles his master, completes the job on an amorous servant-girl, then bashes a blind peasant to pieces.

Throughout these and other excursions into beastliness the dialogue retains a detached courtliness.

Remarks the Baron, after dropping the highwayman's head into the bath:

"Let's have some food, shall we? I'm hungry."

"Pass the marmalade, please," he asks his neglected fiancée at breakfast — while the maid-servant lies mangled upstairs. . . .

The Creature eventually becomes too murderously out-of-hand even for Frankenstein's taste — and gets the acid-disposal treatment itself.

This was short-sightedness on the Baron's part. As the various bodies are unearthed, he has no proof of his story—and so goes to the guillotine himself.

Me, I couldn't raise either a tear or a cheer as the chopper fell. The picture falters uncertainly between two stools of horror:

It isn't quite funny enough to offset moments of nausea.

No tension

It doesn't have sufficient tension or impact to keep your own blood curdled.

The ingredients are on hand, but the camera seems to have taken premature fright.

CHRISTOPHER LEE as the Creature, ROBERT URQUHART as Frankenstein's increasingly-horrified collaborator act excellently within the story's atmosphere.

But Peter Cushing's well-bred, unbending Third Programme approach to madness proved the final defeat of excitement.

You are supposed to pity or loathe Frankenstein, perhaps a little of both.

The one emotion he should NOT arouse is that of irritated boredom.

Long before he was guillotined, Mr. Cushing—mordant, morose and dry—had stifled the life out of Baron Frankenstein.

☆ *Beauty among the horrors. Lovely Hazel Court stars in "The Curse of Frankenstein."*

An adult western

IN THE QUIET GUN Forrest Tucker plays a sheriff who rides out to arrest his best friend for a provoked killing—but is unable to save him from lynching.

This is another, and fairly successful, step in adult direction for Westerns—making a virtue of law-and-order rather than sharp-shooting.

Mr. Tucker continues to make the most solidly satisfying and believable sheriff in the business.

Only a contrived, conventional ending on the "High Noon" pattern mars the picture.

That, plus a recurring gag with an expectant mortician. Even in a Western, jokes about mortuaries are not funny.

LITTLE MISS 'X' SHOCKS FILMLAND

LEE STIERLI. She changed the Censor's mind.

Above Left: Feature in Picturegoer 1957

Above Right: Feature in the Daily Sketch

Opposite Page: Peter Cushing and Hazel

Inset: Hazel being carried by The Creature (Christopher Lee)

The night of our star-studded premiere was a night to remember. No one really knew what to expect. We went dressed in sunglasses and scarves around our heads, incognito, so we could watch the film with the audience without them knowing who we were. There was a great moment during the film when we felt we were a big success – where I'm having breakfast with Peter Cushing. In the previous scene, he was chopping up bodies and dissecting eyes. Then, over the breakfast table, he very gently says, "Please, my dear, pass me the marmalade."

As the audience roared with laughter, off came our sunglasses and scarves. We knew we had a hit. There was tremendous applause at the end of the film, and as we exited the theatre into Leicester Square, hundreds of people were cheering. That was the beginning of a new era of British gothic horror films.

I never knew the film was number one box office in America in 1957. Today, actors and actresses all know where the money goes, but none of us knew a thing of that in those days. We weren't thinking in that direction.

Recently, I ran my video of *The Curse of Frankenstein* and again I was struck by how Christopher Lee was quite remarkable as he managed to infuse sadness into the role and make us feel sympathy for this horrendous-looking creature. Of course, Phil Leakey's makeup is regarded as groundbreaking.

Everyone involved was a highly trained actor, and the sets were excellent. I was most impressed with the real Victorian costumes we had to wear. The director, Terence Fisher, knew his craft and gently steered the production. The film has survived and become a classic.

Watching this movie today brings to mind what is happening with cloning, stem cell research, etc. – things that are even scarier than the movie. The world has caught up with Frankenstein.

THE MAN WHO COULD CHEAT DEATH

My next film for Hammer was *The Man Who Could Cheat Death* (1959), a remake of the 1945 film, *The Man in Half Moon Street* starring Nils Asther. *The Man Who Could Cheat Death* was very interesting but it was not a big success

Above: Scenes from The Man Who Could Cheat Death (1959)

Opposite Page: Publicity Shot

like some of the other Hammer horror films. Many people think that is because there was no Peter Cushing or Vincent Price in the lead – they were the kings of horror.

Anton Diffring was German – a really fine actor who had worked in Germany in all their great theatres. He was charming to work with, but there was a distance in him that was part of his personality. He was fairly serious without a great deal of humour, but very good in the part. He never got the recognition he deserved and was passed over a bit because he wasn't Vincent Price or Peter Cushing. Watching it again recently, I thought, "My God, he is so good – totally right for the part."

I was also reunited with Christopher Lee who was playing the hero this time.

A European version of one scene required me to be naked to the waist as I posed for a sculpture. Appearing topless in a film at that time was very unusual, and I was one of the first in Britain to do so. It was very beautifully shot. The studio was cleared except for only the most necessary personnel for that shot. Only a few people have ever seen the version of the film that has that shot in it. Some still argue that Hammer never shot it at all, but in this book you can see for yourself. We have included a still photo lifted from an original print.

The film is the story of a man played by Anton Diffring who is one hundred and four-years-old at the beginning of the film but looks to be a young man. His partner from school is played by Arnold Marle, a German actor from the famous Berlin school of acting. Marle turns up in the story as an old schoolmate of Anton Diffring, except that he looks his age of eighty-four.

Years before, the two of them had invented an experimental fluid that was the secret to eternal youth – which accounted for the fact that Diffring looked so young, because he had taken it and Marle had not. The fluid was derived from a gland that had to come from the body of a dead person. When Marle arrives on the scene, you see that Diffring's hands are starting to age and he implores Marle to implant the gland in him. Marle initially says, "No, I am not going to do it. Let life be. Let us evolve as we were meant to, not as you are doing, trying to stay eternally young."

In comes this beautiful lady – I can hardly believe it was me! – wearing the most gorgeous dress. I am in love with Diffring's character, really insane about him, and he sculpts me. I had to go to the plasterist at Pinewood Studio for the making of the plaster cast.

Above: Lee, Court and Diffring, The Man Who Could Cheat Death (1959)

As they were slapping on all this plaster onto my bare body, one of them says, "Oh, it's like slapping fish, isn't it? It comes out of the sea, you slap it around on a bench, and then scale it." They were Cockneys and they were so funny.

All that plaster all over me felt terrible, but I kept shouting, "All for art! All for art!" It was a terribly claustrophobic feeling. In the end, after the plaster had set I did say, "Get this off of me, please." It had to be cut off.

The picture evolves that, through a bunch of twists and turns, Diffring kills someone to remove the eternal youth gland and eventually convinces the character played by Christopher Lee, a doctor who is also involved in trying to preserve people's youth, to operate. Diffring is thrilled that he has had the surgery and he will now truly be The Man Who Could Cheat Death. The only thing is, Lee did not really put the gland into Diffring, and at the end of the picture, Diffring is getting old. All kinds of things change in him and he begins to shrivel up. My character, who is a young woman in the story, sees this happening and starts screaming.

The film is very applicable to our times. With the incredible research happening in the medical world today, all the experiments they are doing, and our thirst for the fountain of youth, there is a new reality to these old horror films. It is spooky.

I believe in taking care of yourself and doing things that are good for you. A splash of water on my face before bed, and a little bit of soap and night cream – that is enough. I still smell the fragrance of the rain barrel my mum kept by the back door for washing my face.

I don't believe in cutting your face up to make yourself young again. I am not into that. As for all this business about cutting up the belly to take out the fat, I say, "Yes, let's keep the fat under control, but that belly is where my babies came from. It belongs to them."

THE SHAKEDOWN

After *The Man Who Could Cheat Death* came *The Shakedown* (1959) with Terence Morgan and a star-studded cast including Donald Pleasence, Bill

Owen, and Harry H. Corbett. I had to learn karate for the film. I am told it was one of the first times an actress had tackled karate onscreen, and that my character may have been an inspiration for the female characters in "The Avengers" television series. They were very clever with the way it was shot. After I would finish a karate kick, they cut away from me because I wasn't a karate artist.

"DICK AND THE DUCHESS"

While all of these films were being made, along came the television series *Dick and the Duchess*, a CBS TV series which changed my life. It ran in 1957 and 1958, and preceded my appearances on *Alfred Hitchcock Presents.* The pilot was made in England with an all-British cast except for one American – Ryan O'Neal's cousin, Patrick O'Neal, the leading man.

The producers were Sheldon Reynolds and Nicole Milinaire. Nicole was a very lovely, vivacious, intelligent woman, a divine French lady who became the Duchess of Bedford.

This beautiful pair had made a TV series called *Foreign Intrigue.* It was the first of its kind and an enormous hit, making its producers a big success at CBS in America.

The pilot for *Dick and the Duchess* sold and we were, hopefully, on our way. The series was somewhat unusual in that it was an American sitcom filmed at MGM Studios in Elstree, England, with a primarily English cast and some interesting locations. We had wonderful English character actors and actresses who willingly came in for brief appearances. Margaret Rutherford appeared in my life again, as funny as ever. Ten years later, the "wind" was still there (or in American slang, "gas"), along with cucumber sandwiches by the dozen.

Above Top: Hazel and Patrick O'Neal as Dick and the Duchess (1957-1958)

Above Bottom: (Right to Left) Hazel, director/producer John Foreman and the Duchess of Bedford – Nicole Milinaire, producer Dick and the Duchess (1957-1958)

The show played upon the big differences in expression of the English language, such as, for example, "ironmonger" as opposed to "hardware dealer." As Oscar Wilde said, America and England are "two countries separated by a common language."

Here's the story: The character Dick Starrett, an American, is employed as an insurance claims investigator based in London. He is married to Jane,

HAZEL OFF TO NEW YORK

BIRMINGHAM - BORN actress Hazel Court, who is flying to New York tomorrow evening to make personal appearances in connection with her television programme, "Dick and the Duchess." The film has just been completed at Elstree and is now being shown on American screens.

Hazel, a former Rank starlet, attended Birmingham School of Drama and appeared with Birmingham Repertory Company. The television programme shows her as a comedienne, although her latest film, "Curse of Frankenstein," is now the second-from-the-top box office success in America.

Her seven-year-old daughter, Sally, who plays Hazel as a child in the Frankenstein picture, stays behind with her actor father, Dermot Walsh, who has been starring in the West End of London in "The Kidders."

Above Left: At Sardi's on the night Hazel sees her first Broadway show, My Fair Lady

Above Right: Article in Birmingham Mail

an English woman he affectionately refers to as "the Duchess." Upsetting the apple cart, Jane – guess who? – manages to get herself involved in his claims investigations, trying to help but causing major problems.

We made twenty-six shows, and seemed to be a big success, responsible for two firsts – I wore baby doll night attire which was very sexy and, when kissing Dick in bed, I removed both feet from the floor. Up until then, for TV, we always had to keep one foot on the ground.

I was sent to New York for publicity and promotion for the show. I had never been to America so I was very excited. The plane I flew

EL MOROCC

Previous Page:

Top Left: Hazel and Patrick O'Neal as Dick and the Duchess (1957-1958)

Top Right: Hazel and Eddie Mulhare at El Morocco Nightclub, after seeing Eddie in My Fair Lady

Bottom Left: With Eddie Mulhare and Julie Andrews from My Fair Lady

Bottom Right: Hazel and Eddie Mulhare of My Fair Lady at El Morocco, in New York

This Page: Hazel and Patrick O'Neal

in, the Constellation, was a British Overseas Airways Club plane. It was a marvellous plane with a large plush bar in its belly. We refuelled in Gander, Newfoundland, one of the coldest places I had ever set foot in, although Winnipeg and Chicago come very close.

The plane arrived on time at 6.00 a.m. CBS had sent representatives to meet me and, although I was almost asleep, I showed enthusiasm. Breakfast was in the Berkley Hotel, followed by a press conference. They asked me how I liked New York and wanted me to give my first impressions. I told them that three hours was not enough time for me to form an opinion.

My life was certainly changing. I had to tune in very quickly to the American way of life or I would be lost. My eyes were stinging and I felt sick from lack of sleep, but I knew I must stay upright because I was going to lunch with the president of CBS, Hubbell Robinson, at his country home in Connecticut. I was also going to dinner with the big boss, William Paley, chairman of the board of CBS.

It was truly an exciting time, and my eyes stood out like organ stops. The homes were tremendous, and in the countryside I was treated like a *real* duchess. Hubbell Robinson had heard I told English jokes to the publicity department, so at dinner, I was asked to repeat them. I did, blushing, as I entertained Robinson and his guests.

The whole trip was a big personal success – great publicity, including many magazine covers, and *TV Guide*, of course, where also I made the cover. Skip Shearer of *Parade Magazine*, a delightful man, just loved *Dick and the Duchess* and gave me a wonderful cover story. I was becoming very famous in the U.S. and I was on cloud nine. I understand that *Dick and the Duchess* was President Kennedy's favourite TV show at the time, and that he never missed an episode!

A memorable night was spent with Edward Mulhare who had just taken over from Rex Harrison in *My Fair Lady*. I met a young Julie Andrews and saw my first Broadway show. I loved New York. In one week, I had learnt to speak faster, walk faster, think faster – and to sleep only occasionally. New York is a very exciting city. I would return many times. Life was definitely changing.

HITCHCOCK CALLING

In 1958, my English agent called me and said, "Would you like to go to Hollywood? The Hitchcock show has asked for you."

I was stunned and thrilled, and of course, agreed. It was the third season of *Alfred Hitchcock Presents* and the episode was called "The Crocodile Case." My co-star was the English actor, Denholm Elliot, and my part was excellent. The Denholm Elliot character accidentally reveals himself to the police as the murderer by identifying a crocodile dressing case and the initials engraved on it – details known only by the murderer and the victim.

Within a week, I was on my way to California for the first time. Wide-eyed and excited, I flew to Copenhagen, where I was to catch the night flight to Los Angeles with a Scandinavian airline, SAS Airlines. I will never have a trip like it ever again. Of course, I had a first class ticket but, because it was a night flight, I also had a wonderful bunk bed with fine linen sheets, a soft pillow with SAS embroidered in the corners and what felt like a cashmere blanket. The flight attendant served me hot cocoa and shortbread and wished me goodnight and a comfortable flight.

I've flown the North Pole many times since that night but never in complete luxury again. We go faster now, but in less comfort – no linen sheets. I was awakened the next morning with tea and biscuits.

"Madame," said the flight attendant, *sotto voce*, "please look out of your window, and you will see Greenland in all its grandeur."

Previous Page: Hazel and Hitchcock – Alfred Hitchcock Presents (1955-1962)

Right: Court and Cassidy – Alfred Hitchcock Presents – "The Pearl Necklace" (1961)

There it was – so white and vivid blue. I was looking at a wonderland with an exquisite sunrise painting her way up from dawn. These memories have stayed with me throughout my life. I felt incredibly lucky and rich in experience, discovering the world.

The William Morris Agency representative met me off the plane. His first words were, "Nice to meet you, Miss Court, and welcome to Hollywood. I knew you would be wearing an English suit, tight at the waist." He was right. That was exactly what I was wearing.

Before dropping me at my hotel, he said I must see the famous palm trees of Beverly Hills, and of course, the Beverly Hills Hotel. I felt I was in a movie already, and I was the star. I was given a new script and told I would be picked up at 8.30 a.m. and taken to Universal Studios, where I was to meet the associate producers of the show, Norman Lloyd and Joan Harrison, and the director, Don Taylor.

I had another visitor from the William Morris office. He called to see if I had everything I wanted. His name was Sy Marsh, and he was a wonderful, funny character. I adored him. He asked me if I was nervous, and I said, "Yes!"

"Don't be," he said. "You are going to be directed by one of the nicest men in Hollywood. He will go out of his way to help you and Denholm. He was an actor before becoming a director."

Sy Marsh became my American agent and brought me back to Hollywood three more times.

The next day, I went to the Hitchcock suite of offices at Universal and met everybody. Norman Lloyd and Joan Harrison were delightful people. They were funny, gracious, and made me feel at ease.

I remembered Don Taylor, the director, of course, from his films when he was an actor – *Father of the Bride* with Spencer Tracy and Elizabeth Taylor, *The Naked City* with Barry Fitzgerald, and many more. *The Naked City* was the first time a director shot a film almost entirely on location on the streets of New York. Now, New York streets are always filled with film crews.

Don Taylor was about six foot three inches tall and a very charming, handsome man, with laughter written all over his face. Sy Marsh was right. I would have a good time working with him. Denholm Elliot arrived the next day, and we started rehearsing immediately. Our schedule was three days of rehearsing and three days of shooting. Everything went well. Hitchcock came on the set and asked me if I was enjoying myself.

"Yes, I am," I said.

"Good," he replied. "That's what you're supposed to be doing, Old Bean."

I got all tongue-tied and shy. Here was the great man himself in front of my eyes. His sense of humour was overwhelming. I was never quite sure if he was pulling my leg.

Denholm, a brilliant English actor and a joy to work with, put me at ease. He whispered in my ear. "You and I are as green

Below: Alfred Hitchcock Presents – "The Crocodile Case" (1958)

Above Left and Opposite Page: Alfred Hitchcock Presents – "The Crocodile Case" (1958)

Above Right: Alfred Hitchcock Presents – "The Pearl Necklace" (1961)

as the hills outside, but don't worry. We will have fun and know this country better next time."

The night before, we had got on the freeway going the wrong way. I suddenly looked up and saw San Francisco written on the overhead sign. Yes, we were green all right but laughing a lot about it.

The third day of shooting came to an end, and Don Taylor asked me out for a drink. I had admired him during shooting for his total calm and kindness to actors, so I was intrigued. We talked about everything. Directing was most important to him, except for his two little girls – nine- and ten-years-old – whom he loved very much.

Then it all came out. He was divorcing his wife, Phyllis Avery, a charming actress. He felt little girls should grow up with their mother, and he was going to miss them terribly. He was heartbroken. His pain was very deep.

"Divorce is a horrible creature," I said, "like an octopus with many tentacles." Little did I know that soon I would experience each of those tentacles personally, going through my own divorce from Dermot with all its pain.

Next day, I was on my way home with many memories of Norman Lloyd and Joan Harrison who produced the Hitchcock show as well as anyone possibly could. Not only had I met Hitchcock, the great one himself, but his daughter Pat was in "The Crocodile Case," and we were to become good friends. Pat Hitchcock is a superb lady who has dedicated her life to helping other people and has travelled the world talking about her famous parents. Her mother, Alma, was the great strength behind Hitch.

As we arrived over London, I looked down and saw the River Thames and Windsor Castle. A little shudder went through my body. Somewhere from within, a voice whispered, "Life is changing and will never be the same again."

The next season, I returned to do the Hitchcock show again. The episode, "The Avon Emeralds," was with Roger Moore. Big stars did small parts in those days. Roger was marvellous to work with and very funny – a great raconteur, almost as good as Richard Burton. These were wonderful days of working hard with amazing professional people. So many stars did *Alfred Hitchcock Presents* and gave us so much outstanding viewing pleasure.

In Season 5, I did another episode. This time I was opposite Laurence Harvey, the English actor from *Room at the Top*. The 1959 episode was called "Arthur," and it was rather a nasty little piece – three thousand chickens, Laurence Harvey, a detective and me. Laurence Harvey murders me and loads me into the chicken meal mixture which is then fed to the chickens. Then, the chickens end up roasted for dinner and served to the detective assigned to the case.

Hitchcock said he would like to direct this one himself. We were both highly nervous working with the Great One.

At one point, Hitchcock said to me, "You're supposed to look bad-tempered at this point, Old Bean. You don't have to worry. I shall do it with the camera."

Laurence looked at me and said, "He's only teasing, luv."

On a Season 6 Hitchcock episode, the stars were Jack Cassidy and Ernest Truex. It was called "The Pearl Necklace," and I loved the story and the part. Jack Cassidy played my crooked boyfriend who pushed me into marrying a very rich old man – assuming he would soon be dead. On our first wedding anniversary, my husband rolls an oversized pearl towards me down the baronial table. At the end of the show, I'm sitting again at the baronial table. My elderly husband never did pass on and so, as the show ends, you see me wearing a long, long beautiful set of matched pearls, one for every year of our marriage. It was the only show without a murder and remains one of the most popular.

On top of being a terrible tease – he told funny jokes and dirty jokes – Hitchcock was of course, a true genius. Working with him was an enlightening experience in filmmaking. I believe he could have directed with his eyes shut. An editor at Universal Studios told me that when Hitch was editing his movies, there was very little film left on the cutting room floor. Working with the master was a highlight of my life, even though I'm not so sure he liked actors.

Above: Don Taylor, director, Tom Sawyer (1973)

DON TAYLOR

Don Taylor was working on the next stage and visited me every day. Something was happening beyond our control, and I felt I had known him forever. I was so in love, I couldn't see straight. He made me laugh and he made me cry. Where was all of this going to end up?

Don had a magnificent home in Santa Monica. Charlie, his wonderful golden retriever and best friend, couldn't stand for buttons to remain on furniture and had chewed a giant sofa to pieces. I arrived to find garden furniture now in the living room. Don's divorce was in progress and there was not a great deal left in the house. Don and Charlie shared a bed and pillows.

I met his two little girls, Avery and Anne, ten- and eleven-years-old. They were very attractive, full of life, and possessed their father's sense of humour. The two As – that is how they have remained throughout their lives. Two A-plus girls, very intelligent. Anne – Anne Taylor Fleming – is now a well-known writer. Avery Moore is a marvellous architect.

Above: Don Taylor as Robin Hood in The Men of Sherwood Forest (1954) – a Hammer production

Lee Marvin appeared at the house to stir things up. "So, you're English," he said. The rest of his speech was garbled, so I never got to know what being English meant to him. I can imagine.

Lee was a good friend of Don's, and a marvellously crazy man. Don had directed Lee in the stage production of *Bus Stop*, and they became good friends and drinking buddies. Years later, Don directed *The Great Scout and Cathouse Thursday*, with Lee starring along with Oliver Reed. It was a nightmare. Life was dangerous when Lee was around. And it was no picnic with Oliver either. They both drank like fish. Finally, Don couldn't stand it any longer. "I've had enough of this," he told them. "You must take turns. One of you can drink one day, the other one can drink the next day."

At the end, we had a big farewell cast party on New Year's Eve. Oliver Reed was always a gentleman. He was dressed in a dinner jacket and he was behaving himself. I danced with him, others danced with him. We were all having fun. Out of the blue, he hits the wardrobe master – and breaks his shoulder. Somebody came and whispered in Don's ear, "Get him out of here now." He was taken out of town – and taken home. When he wasn't drinking, he was a lovely man, and the same was true of Lee. They were marvellous actors and both very funny.

I returned to England with mixed feelings. My marriage was not the strongest in the world, but my beautiful little girl, Sally, was waiting for her mum.

THE DODGER GAME

I had been in Los Angeles about a week, working on an episode of the Alfred Hitchcock show when Don Taylor asked me if I would like to go see a Los Angeles Dodgers home game.

"That would be wonderful," I said. "I know nothing about the game. I've never been before."

On a glorious golden California summer evening, we drove through horrendous traffic to Dodger Stadium. I was enthralled by the atmosphere. Fans really loved their game and it was all very exciting. The smell of hot dogs cooking, popcorn popping and cheeseburgers on the grill permeated the stadium. To this day, I love hot dogs with lots of onions, no ketchup.

All was going well. Don had filled me in on how the game was played, and I was intrigued. Leaving me sitting in the stands, he went to get hot dogs. I was quietly enjoying this grand new American adventure when suddenly the people around me stood up. In a blink of my eye, I saw something coming through the air, straight towards me. It was a ball. I shot up, raised my arm into the air, and caught it. Truly the daughter of my father, George W. Court – a well-known cricketer – I had inherited his eye for a catch.

Out of the corner of my eye, I could see Don returning with the hot dogs. "No, no, it's not possible," he yelled out at me, as he dropped the hot dogs.

But it was possible – I had caught the baseball. Everybody around me started to clap and cheer. Of course, I had no idea it was every fan's dream to catch a baseball. Don staggered back to his seat, speechless. My introduction to baseball was very thrilling and became my first big memory of that first visit to Los Angeles – a visit that would, in time, change my destiny.

Below: Hazel, sexy in uniform in Alcoa Theatre – "The Tweed Hat" (1960)

THE ALCOA THEATRE

Don Taylor wrote, directed, and starred with me in an episode of *The Alcoa Theatre* (1960) called "The Tweed Hat."

In the show I am an Englishwoman, and Don plays my American race-car driver husband. The tweed hat is his lucky cap. One day, he dies on the racetrack because he isn't wearing his lucky cap.

In one scene, I am sitting in the living room of the house we had lived in, talking to Don who is already dead. You can hear his voice. He tells me one day I will meet somebody else. I shake my head and wander round the living room. Then it flashes back to the first night we met in England

during the air raids. I was in the Women's RAF in England, and that was where I met him.

At the end of the film I'm in the garden of our house, and a car drives up. A very handsome man asks me to tell him the way to such and such a place. I stare at him for a minute and then point my finger down the lane. "Excuse me," I say, "I don't mean to be rude, but that hat on your head – what does it signify?"

He answers, "That's my lucky cap." As he turns to go, he says, "I'll be seeing you."

As she goes through the door, her husband's tweed hat swings on the peg, and you hear his voice say, "*Auf wiedersehen*, my darling."

The night it aired, the phones were jammed at CBS and at our home. It was a love story and at that time, there were not a lot of love stories on TV. It is a real heartbreaker. It makes you cry.

MEMORIES LIVE LONGER THAN DREAMS: EMBARRASSMENT

Sometimes memories are shrouded in embarrassment, as I learned in the early 1960s when I was invited to Argentina. We were to attend the film festival in Buenos Aires and thought we might even take a side trip to Brasilia. It sounded like a great trip, and I was excited.

It took hours to get from London to Buenos Aires, with a stopover in North Africa. At last we arrived, over-fed and over-wined. Top officials met us, and everything seemed wonderful – until we were told there was a revolution going on. A revolution!

On the way to the hotel, we saw tanks rolling along the streets. The troops were wearing white shirts with large gypsy sleeves and colourful bands draped over their shoulders. They were singing. I didn't really know what it was all about. It gave one the feeling of being in an operetta where, at any moment, the handsome prince would appear.

Finally, we arrived at our hotel. Inside, I rushed to a window and saw the tanks coming down the street and the soldiers from the operetta shooting guns into the sky. It was wild stuff. The parade passed by and all was calm again. Producer/director Michael Powell of *The Red Shoes* and *The Life and Death of Colonel Blimp* fame, was in our party, and he came knocking at my door.

"Did you see it?" he yelled. "It was for real. We came for a film festival and got a revolution!" In his mind, Michael was already writing the script.

We were to meet the press that night, so I got myself glamorously attired and went and knocked on the door of talented English actress Janet Munro who would later die tragically at the age of thirty-eight.

Opposite Page: Hazel and Don Taylor in Alcoa Theatre – "The Tweed Hat" (1960)

Above: Hazel, John Gregson and Janet Munro

"Did you see the revolution?" she yelled through the door.

"No, I saw an operetta," I replied. We roared with laughter as we went off together.

With its wide streets and fantastic shops, Buenos Aires was outstanding. The architecture was intriguing, a mixture of late 1800s and 1900s European. Everything I saw was very stately. Years later, the film *Evita* captured it brilliantly.

We were wined and dined at the highest level, and the ladies were all treated to facials and haircuts. Mine went a little short for my taste. The next day we were going to parade on horseback at the big polo match which was to be attended by the Duke of Edinburgh. My costume was a beautiful pair of sharkskin pants – a fabric that was chic and popular at the time – and a flowing silk shirt made in the blue and white colours of Argentina. As we say in England, I thought I was the cat's whiskers.

Above: Hazel and Janet Munro check in at Airport for Argentina Film Festival

Horses were lined up for us. They were the most tremendous creatures I had ever seen. Their coats were so shiny, I could put on my makeup in the reflection of their gloss. Bands were playing, and the Duke arrived amidst cheers and singing of the British anthem. We were told to mount our horses for the parade. Foot in stirrup, I flung my leg over the horse. A loud cracking sound ripped the air as my beautiful pants split from front to back. I was left with two destroyed halves of a pair of pants, and I was about to cry when a gorgeous gaucho arrived at my side offering me a colourful shawl. I wrapped it around my waist. I was saved. Cheered on by the locals, I made the parade and saluted the Duke as I rode by.

The trip turned out to be wonderful, even with my most embarrassing moment. I decided to bypass Brasilia as Don was waiting for me in California. As it turned out, only Michael Powell made the side trip to that beautiful city. Later, Michael told me I had missed a great experience but, for me, I missed nothing. Love won out over a trip to Brasilia.

SAN VICENTE

Above: Three generations of Taylors – Jonathan, Hazel and Don, Avery Taylor, Grandpa Taylor and Ann Taylor-Fleming at Grandpa Taylor's 91st birthday party

On March 25, 1963, in San Diego, California, I married Don Taylor. We were married by an American Indian named Nathan Wattawa in the presence of two very good friends and talented designers, Hank and Marin Milam. Hank had, for many years, been working on The Valencia Hotel in La Jolla, California and it looked tremendous. That was where we had our wedding breakfast. Later, Don and I travelled to the historic Mission Inn in Riverside, California. The song "A Perfect Day" was written in that inn… *"When you come to the end of a perfect day, and you sit alone with your thoughts, while the chimes ring out with a carol gay, for the joy that the day has brought…"* I was in love and happy. Don enjoyed life so much, and his humour always made us laugh. His dry Scottish sense of humour could have come from his father whose family was from a beautiful little town in Scotland called Crieff.

I remember, shortly after I married Don, we decided we should go back to Freeport, Pennsylvania – a sleepy, charming little town outside Pittsburgh – and present ourselves to his mother and father. One day I looked up at Grandpa Taylor and said, "How did you get from Scotland to here? What made you come to Freeport?"

He looked at me and said, "Well the train stopped here – end of the line."

Grandpa was an engineer and built a number of bridges in Pennsylvania. He was always followed around by tough-looking Mafia types. He would wave his great big walking stick and say, "Get the Sam Hill out of here!" I never knew what the Sam Hill was and I don't know to this day. He died at ninety-three and I was terribly sorry to see him go – a very wonderful man.

The old Santa Monica house we called "San Vicente" was my new home. It was built in 1926 by Don Clark. He was a saxophonist who had played with the Paul Whiteman Orchestra. Mr. Clark saw a wonderful house in England and fell

Right: Hazel at the San Vicente house during her first week in California

Above Left: The San Vicente house

Above Right: Hazel with Jonathan's dog, Blueberry at the San Vicente house during Hazel's first week in California

in love with it. Reproducing that house in Santa Monica, California was a dream come true for him.

His son told me that Bing Crosby made his first recording in the music room of the big house, and many big stars came there to party and have a good time. Don Clark was a great host and, on weekends, his house was the "in" place to drop by. He was too generous and entertained a bit too much, and in the 1930s he was forced to sell his dream house to Mr. Walter Candy, president of Bullock's, a very large department store in Los Angeles.

Don Taylor was in love with the house and had bought it in 1954 or '55, before we married. He had painted it, built a lovely terrace, dug a garden, and caressed it with his very able hands. When I came into his life, he was in the process of pulling it all together after his divorce. To me, I felt that if we were going to make a new start, perhaps it might be a good idea to move away from the area.

"Oh no! I couldn't do that," Don said. "My two little girls live up the street, and I couldn't leave them." They were ten- and eleven-years-old. It seemed healthier to me to be a little bit apart from his old life, but something in my head said "Let it be," so we stayed. I felt it was the right thing to do. I made the decision to incorporate his ex-wife, Phyllis, and their two girls, into our family.

Many years later, when I left San Vicente, Phyllis came over and we had our arms around each other, looking up at the old house. In that house, we had both lived and loved Don. We are still good friends today. I believe that because I did not break up their marriage, my friendship with Phyllis was possible.

My daughter, Sally, had been made a ward of the English courts, and I would not be able to bring her to America for a long time. I missed her terribly. There is always a price to pay in divorce. Eventually, she did come to live for awhile at San Vicente, and it made me very happy.

FOUR WEDDINGS AT SAN VICENTE – AND A FUNERAL

The San Vicente house was powerful, charming, beautiful and very possessive – it ruled our lives. It took a lot of upkeep. Don was always in the garden, always mending the sprinklers. We had a gardener but the work was endless. Even Don's ex-wife Phyllis later said, "Oh my God, this house was so powerful."

Below: Jonathan with Colonel, the Taylor family Irish setter at San Vicente

The forty years I lived there were full of fun living, drama and visits from famous people. We even had four weddings and a funeral – just like the popular movie. The first to wed was Don's youngest daughter, Anne Taylor, to Karl Fleming, a very handsome man, and well-known writer and L.A. bureau chief for *Newsweek*. The wedding was set for the beginning of March and was to be indoors. Having tented the terrace, we all retired for the night, happy about everything. In the middle of the night, the wind bellowed for hours. Next morning – horror upon horrors – only half the tent was there.

Somehow, we got it all together again on time, and a wonderful wedding took place with Anne coming down the aisle to strains of the haunting King Henry VIII ballad, "Greensleeves." As the service ended, Don stood, taking the arm of his first wife, Phyllis Avery on his left, and me, his second wife, on his right. Everybody applauded and cheered. Many, many years later, in an article, Demi Moore said that, as the new modern day family, she and Ashton Kutcher went on holiday and skied with ex-husband Bruce Willis and his wife-to-be, Brook Burns. Move over, Demi. We did it all thirty-five years ago. Christmas, Easter, and birthdays were all shared and enjoyed.

Then my niece, Victoria Barton, married Richard Joy from Grosse Point, Michigan. She was the second bride to tread softly down the aisle at San Vicente. The wedding took place on the front lawn under a beautiful maple tree, and we used the altar Don had built for the first wedding, this time covered in spring flowers. The day was perfect – a California day that sparkles. I remember thinking that the sparkles came from the Pacific Ocean – tiny reflections like silver confetti. Victoria looked absolutely lovely in a white dress that was early Victorian style. As she approached the altar and the vicar began to speak, a bird in the maple tree started to sing. His bird song was stronger and louder than the vicar's. No one could hear a word. Slowly, this wonderful songster got to the end of his wedding hymn and, with a broad smile, the vicar started to speak again.

The bird was quiet, and stayed quiet, until the ceremony was completed, then started again in full throttle. It was all an outstanding experience, helped to perfection by nature.

The third wedding was when Canadian actress, Susan Clarke married Jonathan Taylor's godfather, Robert L. Joseph, a famous writer, producer, and director.

Jonathan Taylor, my son, had been born in 1967. He looked like a Renoir painting, with red hair and sideburns. From the moment of birth, he was on the go. When he was about two-and-a-half years old, I looked out the kitchen window and saw him climbing over an eight-foot chain link fence that went round the swimming pool. He loves everything outdoors, is a great skier and surfer, loves to kayak and collect antiques. He looks after me very well, and the twenty-foot snow banks up here don't seem to worry him at all. A son and a daughter are very important in life. I treasure both my son and my daughter.

Now Jonathan's godfather Bob was getting married. The wedding took place just before Christmas on the terrace of the old house. Of course, the lattice altar was used again, this time covered in holly and mistletoe. Susan was a beautiful bride in a dress I believe was created by the brilliant Hollywood costume designer, Edith Head. The dress was elegant and stunning in its sophisticated lines.

Don's eldest daughter Avery married Tom Moore on the front lawn – and we had our fourth wedding. Two bridesmaids – her sister Anne, and my daughter

Sally – attended her. Chairs were set in two semicircles, the aisle down the middle leading to the now- famous altar that Don built. Avery sailed down the aisle in a white halter-neck dress, simple but stunning, three delicate gardenias caressing her pretty ash blonde hair. The music was strangely stirring and very beautiful, setting the whole tone of the wedding. With the sun shining, and bridesmaids dressed in pastel chiffon, it was a romantic, happy wedding. The swirling happy atmosphere lingered long into the evening when the blue-gray California dusk began to settle, and a new moon appeared over the old house.

After four weddings, then a funeral. To my great sadness, Robert Joseph has left us. He was a very special man.

MEMORIES LIVE LONGER THAN DREAMS: HOLLYWOOD PARTY

It was my first Hollywood party, at the home of John Swope, a very famous photographer. My husband Don seemed to know everybody. "Hi Bob. Hi Joe," and so on. As for me, I was feeling overwhelmed by the Hollywood scene. Suddenly a hush fell over the room, and people were getting in a long line from the front door to the terrace.

"What's going on, Don?" I asked.

"Who knows?" he laughed.

"The Queen of England isn't in town by any chance?" I joked.

Gliding through the front door was Judy Garland, looking wonderful and fabulous. It was the dream of my life to meet *the* great Judy Garland as I had always envisioned her. Every famous star has extraordinary eyes, penetrating and overflowing with creativity. Elizabeth Taylor has this quality.

Judy Garland's eyes were almost overwhelming. She also possessed great charm and warmth, shaking hands and talking with everyone.

When she got to Don and me, she screamed to her husband, Sid Luft, "Sid, it's the Duchess!"

She grasped my hand and vigorously shook it. "You gave my husband and me such pleasure watching you in your TV show," she said. "When I was on the road with my show, I would watch you between the matinee and evening shows. You are a wonderful comedienne and you made me laugh. Keep making people laugh. It's a great gift to have." As she passed, her hand squeezed my shoulder. "Lovely to meet you, Duchess."

I was about to pass out. There was no time to tell her that for the little girl from Birmingham, England, standing beside her, my dream had come true. There she was, saying, "I'm so glad to meet *you*."

Don was very impressed. No more "Hi Bob. Hi Joe." He was just hugging and loving me.

Memories do live longer than dreams. There is a little more substance to the memories.

Above: Hazel and Pernell Roberts in Bonanza – "The Last Trophy" (1960)

SURPRISE GUESTS

I was returning home from somewhere and as I shut the front door, I heard raucous laughter from the kitchen area, and it was a laugh I did not recognise. I went to investigate the great smells coming from the kitchen.

Anne and Avery Taylor were entertaining. "Hi Haz, we're cooking hamburgers."

Some of the young people I knew, but one person was a stranger.

"Haz," said Anne, "I think you know everybody except Bill Clinton."

I shook hands with a tall man with a shock of black curly hair – a lot of it. He looked like a pom-pom. He was somewhere in his twenties, with a face full of mischief. He seemed charming and ready for wild fun. Little did I think this black pom-pom would become president of the United States.

He still loves hamburgers, his favourite food. Born a Leo in August, it's no surprise. They love meat. My son is a Leo, so I know.

Surprise guests are often very interesting and unforgettable.

MORE TV MEMORIES

Apart from the sorrows, life was very exciting. Hollywood was still Hollywood. Working in the studios still had grace and dignity. It was always fun to go to work. I was acting, and Don was directing. Television was just blossoming. After *Alfred Hitchcock Presents*, I did a lot of good work, like *Bonanza*, *The Wild Wild West*, *Dr. Kildare*, *Gidget*, and *The Twilight Zone*.

On *Dr. Kildare* I found Richard Chamberlain to be a very professional, very good actor. He loved the theatre and, after *Dr. Kildare*,

This and Opposite Page: Hazel and Pernell Roberts in Bonanza – "The Last Trophy" (1960)

he did go to work in the theatre and also played the part of the priest in *The Thorn Birds*. I was never sure in that show whether it was him I actually found so attractive in that part, or simply the idea of a priest falling in love with a woman.

In 1964, I did an episode of *The Twilight Zone* entitled "The Fear." It was written by Rod Serling and directed by Ted Post. Rod Serling was a wonderful human being – very handsome – and he flirted like mad. I remember him saying one day, "I won't live to old age. My father died young of a heart attack." He turned out to be right.

The episode is about fifty-foot tall giants that come to earth. They can lift cars with one hand. I play a fashion editor who is sad about her life and goes to live in the mountains. Along comes Peter Mark Richman who plays a state trooper. Peter Mark Richman was very handsome, but his was not an American-looking face.

"Are you all right?" he asks.

At first I am very rude to him, but he is so nice to me that I soften. "I called the police," I explain, "because something is going on here. I heard sounds on the roof."

He goes to check it out, and returns, saying, "No, Ma'am, everything is fine here."

Then he goes and looks at his car and sees footprints the size of a house. The next thing he knows, his car has been moved.

"My car was moved by people who must have been fifty feet tall!" he reports.

“I’m getting out of here,” I say.

“No, I will stay the night and watch over you,” he promises.

After finding these enormous footprints in the earth, and discovering that his car has been moved back, he tells me that something weird is definitely going on.

As we stand there looking at the car, I say, “I’m getting out of here. I’m going to the village.” We are running to get into the car to make our getaway, and we see the giant up ahead.

I will let Peter Mark Richman himself finish the story. Quoting him from a recent “Twilight Zone Roundtable” assembled by Twilight Zone writer George Clayton Johnson, Peter Mark says, “Finally we see this huge eight-storey monster, and I’m going to pop him off with a gun. I do and the thing fizzles down to a big balloon. We look through the balloon window and it is miniature tiny aliens from outer space.”

That same year, I also did an episode of *Rawhide* starring Clint Eastwood. I found him to be a very isolated figure. He has become such a talented director, has lived a good long life, and is still going strong.

Looking back, life was full of stories. One of my favourite experiences was while working on *Sam Benedict* with Edmond O’Brien who treated us to scenes from Shakespeare throughout the day. It was a courtroom story, and there was a scene where he used the desk as a platform, jumping on top of it and giving us *Hamlet, Richard I, Richard III* and all the rest. I played a great part – a beautiful pathological liar who fooled everyone. Richard Donner (*Lethal Weapon*) directed us. We had a wonderful time.

I remember *Bonanza* because it was one of the first episodes. Everyone was fresh and so full of enthusiasm. They were a great team – Dan Blocker, Pernell Roberts, Michael Landon and Lorne Green. Michael Landon was truly nice and full of fun. It always seems to me in looking back, he really died before his time. Dan Blocker died before his time, too. My first day was very memorable. The first shot of the day was me on a horse alongside Pernell Roberts. Pernell told me that his horse and mine were stable mates and did everything together. As Pernell moved away, my horse took off after his. I was not ready for it, and was thrown sky high.

The first assistant rushed up to the director and yelled, “The English Missy has fallen off her horse.” The director yelled back, “Have you got the horse?” Teasing me was a big part of their day, and I had a wonderful time with them all. We had lots of laughs and good memories.

Above: Hazel and Peter Mark Richman in The Twilight Zone – "The Fear" (1964)

Working on *The Wild Wild West* with Sammy Davis Jr., Peter Lawford and Robert Conrad was a great experience. Sammy was a very kind and warm-hearted star, a delightful person, full of humour. I remember being on the set, reading "Renoir, My Father," by Renoir's son, Jean. I could not put it down.

Sammy shouted across the floor, "Hazel, what is more interesting than me?"

"Renoir," I yelled back, "the famous painter."

That was enough. Sammy took the book from my hands and started tossing it around the set like a football.

Peter Lawford, who I liked very much, came and sat beside me. I had become very friendly with him and found in him a much deeper person than he presented to the public.

To my surprise, he sank into his chair and said with an enormous sigh, "What the hell are we doing in this profession?"

I really enjoyed him, and he tried to get me into his series *The Thin Man*. He also tried to arrange for me to have dinner with Jack Kennedy, who had enjoyed my *Dick and the Duchess* TV series. I knew Don would not go along with it, so I declined the introduction. Peter was caught in the web of the Kennedys and was never his true self. He had wandered off the track and could never get back on.

One of my sad TV memories was from *Mannix* starring Mike Connors. I had been asked to guest star along with Michael Wilding, who I knew from doing *Carnival* many years before. He was as charming as he could have been, and he still looked good, but since he could not remember his lines, I held a card with the script on it. His embarrassment saddened me terribly. When actors can't remember their lines, it digs into the heart. It made me worry that someday that could be me.

DR. BLOOD'S COFFIN

Dr. Blood's Coffin (1961) was a very spooky film to make. It was directed by Sidney Furie who, among many other stellar credits, went on to direct *Superman IV: The Quest for Peace*. On the Internet Movie Database he is quoted as saying, "The truth is, whether your film is about the great mythological character you have to do right, or it's a little movie that nobody ever heard of, you still approach it like it's the most important thing in the world. But failing goes with the territory. Filmmakers are like gunslingers, and you don't win every duel."

The film starred Kieron Moore and Ian Hunter. Set in a very old village on the beautiful rugged coastline of Cornwall, England, Dr. Peter Blood believes he can create the perfect human being. Beneath the ocean in abandoned mines, he has built himself a secret laboratory. The villagers become suspicious when suddenly a number of people are missing. Dr. Blood was in need of hearts.

It was wild, going into the mines under the ocean, disused for many, many, many years. We accessed the disused mines from the rocks along the coastline. It was very scary. At one point, I looked up and whispered to myself, "Oh my God, the Atlantic Ocean is above me." As I have said many times, Cornwall is a mystical, magical place loaded with legends and pixies.

As I write this, it occurs to me that I always seem to be in horror movies about making dead men live again. Perhaps the message is that life goes on, regardless.

Left: Hazel and The Monster from Dr. Blood's Coffin (1961) (Filmed beneath the Atlantic Ocean)

THE PREMATURE BURIAL, A ROGER CORMAN FILM

The Premature Burial (1962) was a strange movie. Directed by Roger Corman, the film starred Ray Milland. It was written by esteemed writer Charles Beaumont and based upon the story by Edgar Allen Poe. It is interesting to note that Francis Ford Coppola, not yet renowned, was Assistant Director on the picture.

The Edgar Allen Poe story upon which the film was based is about the fear of being buried alive – and it got to us all. The fear was very personal for Poe, who suffered from it all of his life. It was a good part for me, with gorgeous clothes and great camera work. There is a scene near the beginning of the film in which I'm playing the piano at our post-wedding gathering. My daughter Sally is the true pianist in the family. I can only play a little bit, so I played a few bars of Tchaikovsky's piano concerto and substituted that in place of the actual piece of music I was supposed to be playing.

I was very excited about working with Ray Milland. He had won an Oscar for his performance as the alcoholic Don Birnam in the Billy Wilder film *The Lost Weekend*. He was tremendous in that movie. Being Welsh, he wrote outstanding poetry, and being half Welsh myself, I loved talking to him.

There is a scene in which I burst in upon my husband in his art studio, and I insist on seeing the canvas he is working on. He acquiesces, but says something like, “You won’t find it very pleasant.” Then he whips off the fabric that is covering his painting and reveals a painting which was actually done by a very interesting artist, Burt Schonberg, who is also

Above: Hazel and Roger Corman, The Premature Burial (1962)

credited with having his paintings in another picture based upon a Poe story, *The House of Usher*.

At the end of the picture, I had to be buried alive. Roger asked me if I would do it or if I would rather have someone double for me. I said, “Heaven’s no! I will do it.” Well, I lay in the ground, with a straw in my mouth so that I would have air, as they shovelled the earth over me. The straw was removed when the director said, “Action!” I was to hold my breath for as long as possible. I made it for over one minute – long enough to get the shot. As I got to the end of the minute, the pressure on my body began, as the claustrophobia was setting in. It was one hell of an experience.

Left: Hazel in publicity shot for The Premature Burial (1962)

Above: With Richard Ney from the same film

This Page: Milland and Hazel – The Premature Burial (1962)

Also by the end of the film, I think the whole idea of being buried alive really got to Ray Milland. While we were making the film, he kept asking questions along the lines of, "Oh my God, could we really be buried alive?"

Richard Ney played Miles in the film. We had a wonderful relationship. In real life, he was married to Greer Garson. The marriage was a studio thing – it was time for him to be married. In those days, they might say to you, "Time to run off and be married now." *The Premature Burial* was his last picture. While making the film, he found that he loved playing the stock market. Suddenly, he was making a lot of money. One day he told me he was thinking of giving up acting. He did, and I'm told he became very rich.

Heather Angel, a very beautiful actress from the fifties, was also in the film. So was Alan Napier, a delightful man who always looked as if he was off to play cricket.

The Premature Burial was not as successful as the other horror films. Some critics felt it was because Vincent Price was not in it. I felt it might have been because a lot of people have fears of being buried alive – or of developing the condition of catalepsy in which one would be alive but accidentally presumed dead. The film was kind to me, and as I've mentioned, a very good part.

THE RAVEN, A ROGER CORMAN FILM

The Raven, another film directed by Roger Corman, written by Richard Matheson – an esteemed writer who was a contemporary and friend of Charles Beaumont – and based upon a story by Edgar Allen Poe, was sheer joy. Working with Vincent Price, Boris Karloff, and Peter Lorre was quite a challenge, and it was a rare occasion for an actress to be working with those three giants at the same time. The teasing and laughter that went on was too much. One day, Roger said, "I'm going back to California and I'm going to take a course at UCLA on how to handle actors." He did a wonderful job of controlling these three actors, all fighting to be the top dog.

Above: Lobby Card from The Raven (1963)

On all these films I made for Roger Corman, we got a script, we rehearsed, and we went into production. He was a fast director, and we

Above: Boris appreciates Hazel's assets in The Raven (1963)

Opposite Page: Court cuts up in The Raven (1963)

worked very quickly. It was all over in four weeks. Roger was very, very clever. He went on to do some very interesting foreign films, and other things. He was wonderful to work for, always allowing us to do our thing on set, to be ourselves and make jokes.

We were directed to do the work. There were never any tantrums, no questions, no posturing, and no stardom. It went as a day-to-day job. I don't know why it takes so long to make a film these days. It is beyond me. Those films cost $200,000 to make, and they were beautifully presented – including the sets and the real Victorian costumes.

Throughout the years, I wore so many beautiful Victorian gowns, really gorgeous. They came from Moss Brothers, the costume place. It is funny, but when you get into an old costume, one almost takes on the vibes of the costume, particularly with my imagination.

I spent years in repertory theatre, and I was trained to move well in those costumes. I was in a touring company with Dermot, doing play after play, and we were taught to walk in the style of the period. In Victorian days, they walked stiffly because of the dresses and the crinoline. Don't forget, we were wearing real corsets. They give you wonderful support and a certain dignity. Every time I wore a corset, it brought to mind the corset lady from my youth who always came in the Spring to visit my mother.

Peter Lorre had a background in theatre in Berlin, Germany, which he seemed to be very proud of, but he told me he felt Hollywood had never given him a proper chance at comedies. He was always cast in dramas, so he adored his part in *The Raven*. He was very funny and warm. When he was fitted with the "raven" wings, he went crazy, flying around the set, waving them like a helicopter, tickling Vincent's nose and screaming, "I'm a bird."

Jack Nicholson kept popping around, saying "I'm going home to write tonight," but he never told us what he was writing. I think this was among the first films he did. Looking at him today on film, it is hard to believe he was in *The Raven*, wearing medieval pantaloons. They did not suit him at all, but he had enough personality to overcome them.

Boris was very charming, a real English gentleman – soft, gentle, and polite. He was nothing like the parts he played. He was a magnificent storyteller. In fact, all three of them were great raconteurs. All three of them also had great art collections, and I felt that they all enjoyed each other and were happy to be together. Between the three of them, their art collections could have filled the Metropolitan Museum of Art.

I got to know Vincent Price really well, and of course, we talked about art a great deal. I didn't tell him that I painted. It would have been like, "Come up and see my etchings." One day, he did come back to the house for a drink. Don had hung two of my paintings in the living room.

"Who did those?" Vincent yelled.

"Hazel," Don said.

"Don't be silly," Vincent replied. "Who really did them? I want to know because I would love to buy them."

"I did them," I assured him. "I really did."

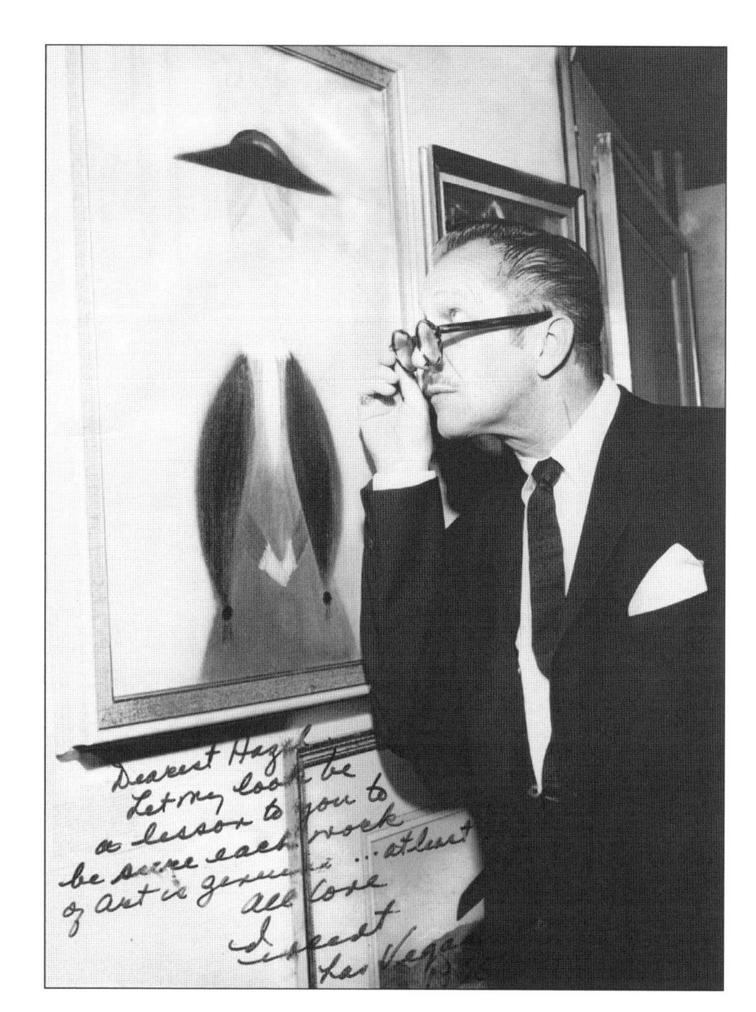

Above Left: Vincent Price at the San Vicente house checking Hazel's painting

Above Right: Boris and Hazel in The Raven (1963)

Well, to cut a long story short, he did buy one, and in fact many more, for his famous Sears and Roebuck Collection. He supported my work through the following years, and wanted me to give up acting to travel the museums of Europe. I wasn't quite ready, but it did come to pass.

The joy of watching these wonderful stars together was a highlight of my life. Never any trouble, they were very humble, with no conceit about who they were. It was a marvellous romp from start to finish with Roger Corman being in charge of these powerhouses. Roger was young and handsome, with great energy, and he knew how to use the stars' friendly rivalry for the good of the film. Thank you, Roger, for such a tremendous experience. You used magic, and made the film such fun.

There is a delicious scene in which I gleefully say, "Are we going to have some torture?"

The scene I loved the most was at the very end where Karloff and I get blown up. Somehow I survive and come up the chimney looking slightly cockeyed. Then I get pounded by Vincent with debris made of a fibrous substance, while Vincent is laughing his head off, and Lorre as the Raven is screeching. "Serves you right."

Quoth the Raven, "Nevermore."

THE MASQUE OF THE RED DEATH, A ROGER CORMAN FILM

The Masque of the Red Death, another well-made film based upon a story by Edgar Allen Poe, was the third in the trilogy I did with Roger Corman – and one of Roger Corman's most successful Poe horror films. It was also written by Charles Beaumont, the writer of The Premature Burial. This film is often on television. American Movie Classics (AMC) and Turner Classic Movies (TMC) have paid tribute to the production many times.

Below: Hazel in Masque of the Red Death (1964)

I remember reading in a magazine about the film. They wrote something to the effect of, "Roger Corman made good use of the standing set from Becket [the Peter Glenville film starring Richard Burton and Peter O'Toole] and was able to produce this film in a mere six weeks. The production values are top notch and the acting is good for its budget, especially Price." Also, "As with many of his Poe productions, this film actually combines a number of Poe stories, two of which are [the poem] 'Hop Frog' and [the story] 'Red Death.' With this film, Roger Corman would deliver his best of the Edgar Allen Poe series. Acting nods to Hazel Court, who almost upstages Price. A recommended delight." (Bracketed information added.)

Roger did an outstanding job of directing *The Masque of the Red Death*, which critics have described as "the most Bergman-like of Corman's films, an ultra stylish adaptation of the Poe tales." The film was woven into a rich tapestry by lavish costumes, artfully designed sets, and of course, a great cinematographer – Nicolas Roeg, who later became a wonderful director. His film *Don't Look Now*, set in Venice, starring Donald Sutherland and Julie Christie, became a classic.

Jane Asher, who played Francesca in the film, had fallen madly in love with Paul McCartney while

Above: The famous branding scene from Masque of the Red Death (1964)

interviewing him the year before *The Masque of the Red Death*. They began a relationship at that time which would last five years, resulting in an engagement, and inspire many Lennon/McCartney songs, like "Here, There, and Everywhere," "I'm Looking Through You," "You Won't See Me," "We Can Work It Out," "And I Love Her," and "For No One." Her brother was Peter of the duo Peter & Gordon, who recorded the Lennon/McCartney hit "A World Without Love."

One day I saw her knitting on the set. "Whatever is that?" I asked, looking at the item she was knitting.

"Oh," she said, "it's a Balaclava helmet. I'm knitting one for each of the Beatles so they can go out at night and not be recognized. I'm in love with Paul, you know, and I'm going to marry him." (For those of you wondering, a Balaclava helmet is a ski-like woollen mask that pulls on and covers the whole head, with openings either for the whole face or just for the eyes.)

"I think someone sixteen or seventeen years old such as yourself, with all your talent, may be too young to make that big a decision, dear," I replied.

She did not marry Paul. She went on to become a wonderful actress and writer, and opened her own cake shop in London, which became quite famous. She designs and ices her exquisite cakes, and no matter what you want – even if it is the Tower of London – on top of your cake, she will do it. She is a very gifted and successful lady who, in a very un-showbiz way, ended up marrying the English cartoonist/illustrator Gerald Scarfe who is best known for his creation of cover art for a Pink Floyd album. They have three grown children, and her home life remains very important to her, and very private.

Vincent Price played Prospero, the Prince of Darkness, and I played the lady who gave herself to the devil. Prince Prospero rules from his castle on the hill, sure that the Red Death will not get him. The whole movie was a delight.

The scenes in the film where I sacrifice myself to the devil gave me a very strange feeling. It was almost like I was really doing it, and I thought, "Oh my God, I am giving myself to the devil!"

In one scene, I enter the room where Jane Asher is, and I have a mark on my breast. She says, "What's that?" and I say, "Satan's mark."

"Prospero did that to you?"

"No, I did it to myself," I reply. "It marks me as one of Satan's

Above Top: A scene from Masque of the Red Death (1964)

Above Bottom: Jane Asher and Hazel in Masque of the Red Death (1964)

This Page and Opposite: Masque of the Red Death (1964)

handmaidens." And then I shudder. It really did give me a cold chill. Once I have sacrificed myself to Satan, I go into a trance-like state where I am floating, but even that scene, in which I have to writhe around screaming on a cold slab, did not affect me like stabbing my breast and giving myself to the devil. "…Together on earth we shall live as man and wife and when he calls us, you shall be Satan and I, still, your wife…"

As I walk toward the swinging pendulum of the clock, and I am in that state of reverie, you don't expect the raven to attack me – the Bird of Death I called him.

Working with Roger was a joy. He was so easy to be around, and he put up with all of us misbehaving.

Vincent I knew very well by now. We had made The Raven together, and my husband, Don Taylor, was very good friends with him. He was a sheer delight – very kind, funny, and with a wonderful mind which would move from grand humour to being very serious and deep, in an instant if need be. Each hour I spent with him I learned a great deal.

Opposite Page:

Top: Hazel, Cecil Kellaway and Dick Powell in The Dick Powell Show – "A Swiss Affair" (1961)

Bottom: Hazel and Peter Graves in Mission Impossible – "Charity" (1967)

Vincent was always joking and having fun, telling wild stories in our ears. None of this ever affected his work, for he was ever and always a professional. Even when he was playing a disturbing role, he never frightened me.

Near the beginning of the film, there is a scene where this darling little ballerina is dancing for the entertainment of Prince Prospero. She misses a step, and Prospero slaps her across the face. It is a shocking moment, and so far from Vincent's actual personality. There was no coldness in him. I knew that he was one hundred percent laughter, but he did have this brilliant switcheroo he would do – this tremendous ability to be smiling and charming one minute, looking at you with adoring eyes, and the next minute viciously stabbing someone. I think he had a bigger impact because he had so much warmth in him, and then he'd make that wonderful switch. At the end, even after he had cut somebody up, he would crack a joke.

The last week of his life, he bought a small painting from an unknown artist. That was wonderful Vincent. He did not have the shaking that many people with Parkinson's disease have, but the illness made his life miserable because it made him unable to move at will.

The last time I went to see Vincent, Don was about to take me to a Miró art exhibition at the Museum of Modern Art in New York.

"I hope I enjoy the exhibition, Vincent. I don't always understand Miró's work."

"Don't worry," he said, "when you get back, dear girl, I will explain a lot to you about Miró. I adore him."

Vincent died at the exact moment I was walking through that exhibit. His joy in life was enormous and infectious, and his death was a great loss to me. He was one of those people in one's life that you think will always be there. And he is – in spirit.

FAVOURITE FILM AND TV MOMENTS

One of my funniest experiences was in the English TV series, *The Buccaneers* on an episode called "Gentleman Jack and the Lady." In the episode, I played both the part of Anne Bonney and Gentleman Jack. Because I was playing the part of a male pirate, they told me, "You've got to speak with a deep voice." I did speak like a man, but it didn't really come across with my voice, so they dubbed me in the end.

The film I enjoyed making the most was *The Raven* because I am the only female to have acted in a film with the three greats together – Boris

Karloff, Peter Lorre, and Vincent Price. It was fascinating to listen to all three of them talk and challenge each other every day. Being with the three of them, as they kept trying to outdo each other, was wonderful.

My favourite of all the TV shows I was in would be *Four Star Playhouse* with Dick Powell, Charles Boyer, David Niven and Ida Lupino. I did two of them, one with an actor called John Payne and one with Dick Powell. In one of the episodes, called "The Swiss Affair," the photography was so good. I ran into someone who had recently run "The Swiss Affair" and they said, "Oh God, you kept us guessing. We kept saying, 'It's not Hazel, it's not,' but it turned out to be you after all." I have been told I have a kind of innocence in my face, a sweetness, and no one expects it when I turn out to be venomous.

Dick Powell, a super human being, introduced *Four Star Playhouse* every night. He died just after he made this show which was a remake of *My Favourite Spy* with Madeleine Carroll, one of the most beautiful creatures I've ever seen. Her time was in the 1930s and 1940s. I met her once for lunch many, many years later in her life and she was still incredibly beautiful. She married a man in the French resistance with scars on his face. He was the most handsome man in the world and the only man I've ever seen where the scars made him more handsome.

My favourite location shoot was on *Five Man Army* (1969) which Don was directing in Italy. It was a wonderful film, absolutely marvellous. I wasn't in the film, but I went along because we were going to live on the Appian Way. Jonathan was a little one at the time. Those were the days of Sophia Loren, and Rome was at its height. With all the films being made there, it was known as Taylor-Burton country. We were filming in Rome right after Liz Taylor and Richard Burton made *Cleopatra* there. They lived on the Appian Way in an old farmhouse, and we visited their favourite romantic restaurant, Hostaria-L'Archeologia, and I bought twelve of their wine glasses. I have one left.

The film starred Peter Graves, whom I had met on "Charity," an episode of *Mission Impossible* from 1967. I instantly liked Peter. Don and I were in Italy for six months with Peter and his wife Joan, and the four of us had a ball. We were in Rome most of the time, but we travelled all over – North, South, East, and West – and we went to every antique store. We all laughed a lot and lovely things happened when we were together.

I am still friendly with Peter Graves and his wife. They have a place up here. I used to say I would love to have a log cabin, and it was Joan Graves who rang up one day and said, "I think I have found you a log cabin." She found this place that looks to the mountains, with its Japanese architecture that looks like a set from *Madame Butterfly*.

McMillan and Wife with Rock Hudson was memorable. He was very pleasant to work with and very nice, but there was always a shield around him. *Bonanza* made me laugh the most because the other actors never stopped teasing me. They never let up.

In 1965, I was working with Richard Chamberlain on the *Dr. Kildare* show at MGM Studios. We worked very fast, and it seemed to me I was always running from set to dressing room, and back again. One particular day, I was running *very fast* to get back on the set. Not looking where I was going, I bumped pretty hard into someone – a kind of bounce off a stomach. Looking up to this person's face, I was stunned to see it was Elvis Presley.

"Hey, where are you going in such a hurry?" he laughed.

"I'm trying to get on my set, 'Dr. Kildare.' I'm working here."

His face was magnificent, very handsome and powerful, and there was an energy all around him. I found him riveting.

"When are you finishing today?" he asked.

"Oh, I'm working all night," I hurriedly said. "Please let me pass."

With a dark twinkle in his eye he said, "I'm working here, too. Maybe we will bump into each other again."

I squeezed past him. "Lovely to have met you, Mr. Presley," I said in a small voice. "Goodbye." Fleeing down the corridor, I turned around. He was laughing as he waved one of those famous hands. I will never forget the energy that surrounded him, even as he waved. Mesmerising. I should have gone back and talked, but I was very young.

Those days were the end of the great days of Hollywood where we worked with very intelligent people, and everyone was pleasant and mannered. When you went to another country on location, people would look after you. They would call and ask, "Are you all right? Do you need anything? Can we do anything for you?"

By 1967 or so, everything in Hollywood had already started to change.

LIFE BEGAN TO CHANGE

At the beginning of May 1980, my life began to follow a whole different path. For awhile, my dear friend Diana Basehart – the wife of the lovely talented actor Richard Basehart – had been teaching me to sculpt in stone. Diana was a renowned sculptor in her own right. One day while I was watching her work, she put a file in one of my hands and a piece of alabaster in the other. She said with great sincerity, "I do believe you could sculpt, Hazel." I was amazed but thrilled at the same time, and that was the beginning of my exciting entry into the magnificent world of carving.

Above: Hazel at work in Sculpture Studio in Pietrasanta, Italy

The next step down that road came in the form of a phone call from Bernice McMann, a lovely friend who was also a very talented sculptor.

"Would you like to go to Italy to sculpt?" said a teasing voice.

"What do you mean?" I asked.

"Well, there is a lady called Bernice Schachter who teaches sculpture and takes a group to Pietrasanta, Italy every May, June and July. Two spots are available in May but to get accepted, we must be quick."

It all sounded too good to be true. The next day while thinking about this new expansion to my life, I came to the conclusion that I had nothing to lose by trying. Mrs. Schachter could only say "yes" or "no." So, on a rain-sodden day soaked in gloom, I packed up a piece of my work and departed to Bernice Schachter's studio in the San Fernando Valley in California. I was immediately impressed with this tall, strong, very good looking lady. I was showing her my work, and asking if it was good enough to join her class in Italy.

"Your work is excellent," she said. "I would enjoy having you."

Above: Hazel at work in Sculpture Studio in Pietrasanta, Italy

In that moment, it was hard to imagine that someone would ever write of my work, “Having studied art for nearly thirty years, I am truly impressed with this artist’s capacity to give life to stone, transcending reality without denying it.” That quote was from Gwynne Galleries’ owner Lee Mestres. It was so kind.

I was on my way to a new adventure. We all flew to Rome – Bernice McMann, Deta Spatz, and Ernestine Voss. Bernice Schachter was already in Italy, preparing for the class. On the plane, Bernice McMann had her birthday and said it was the best birthday she had ever had. She was a delight, and a good time was had by all.

Changing planes in Rome, we caught a plane to Pisa, where we drove to Pietrasanta. The town was founded in the thirteenth century, and part of the Roman wall still exists there. During the fifteenth century, the town grew to importance, mainly due to its connection to marble. Michelangelo had lived there when he carved the famous pieta, and he was the first to appreciate the beauty of the local stone. The famous sculptor Botero keeps a residence there today. Also, Henry Moore sculpted there. Driving in this marvellous old town was magical.

The meeting place for all the sculptors was a large square, and the impressive duomo, where Michelangelo had worshipped, was the master of the square. Life was a divine dream with more to come.

Our hotel, The Italia, was probably built in the 1920s and, while it had great character, it needed loads of paint and a lot of attention. There was no comfort there, but everybody was happy as we climbed the stairs to our spartan rooms. Water chugged loudly as it came out of the tap. When one flushed the toilet, it could be heard all over the hotel. The shower sprayed itself all over the bathroom floor – and the toilet paper rolls never escaped the spray. It was all like being back at school.

Ivano Stampeggi, the charismatic character who ran the hotel, spoke seven languages and was full of fun. Isabel, his beautiful wife, was English.

At eight o'clock breakfast the next day, Bernice Schachter explained the life we would be leading for the next month. "Do any of you have any questions?" she gently approached.

"Yes, what about the traffic noise?" we all wanted to know.

"I have the solution in my pocket," she said, and out shot a whole fistful of earplugs, making all of us laugh.

FIRST DAY AT THE SILVERIO STUDIO

About a quarter of a mile from the hotel was the great studio where Silverio Paulo reigned supreme. It was to Silverio Paulo's studio that Bernice Schachter would take sculpture students every year. We each had our own compressor and table, and Silverio would provide all the materials and the assistants. Silverio's son, Marco, ran the studio, lifting, polishing, and cutting marble.

Adjoining the medieval wall was a lovely garden with peach and olive trees and an array of flowers. Two turtles and four cats roamed round – Michelangelo was a black and white beauty. His joy in life was to curl up on the sculptures and tell us stories with a high-pitched purr. Life was great and we were having an extraordinary experience. Those magical times with all their special qualities have stayed with me for so many years.

Diana Basehart's mother Gwyneth, a wonderful artist and writer, wrote at the age of ninety-seven:

Hold, caress, turn and turn some more, this solid rough-angled piece of stone. Let your mind, your eyes, your senses soar, seeing some beautiful form that you will not ignore. Then, if you can make this solid rock bend, twist and turn in glorious lines, you will have created your masterpiece for all time.

That quote sort of captured the experience for me. I, myself, once remarked, "The joy of bringing alive the spirit of stone is one of the most satisfying fulfilments of my life. I shall run out of time, but nature's glorious shapes shall be here forever."

Pieces of my work are displayed in San Francisco and New York, in England and Taiwan and, after talking to the Fine Arts Department at Sierra Nevada College, I recently had a piece of my sculpture accepted for display in their new Environmental Building. The school has a tremendous emphasis on digital art and entertainment technology.

The piece will be placed in the brand new Tahoe Center for Environmental Sciences, a building that is a research facility for issues related to the environment. My sculpture will be on the ground floor of the building where there is a lake and a research boat built for demonstration purposes. As soon as I saw the entrance lobby, I said, "That's the place to put it. That's where it is going to go."

You can walk up and get a virtual demo from a virtual lab technician on the boat. There are many such demos throughout the building.

My sculpture is of a fish fossil and is made of black Italian marble with flecks of natural silver running through it. The piece links both the arts on which the college was founded and the institution's environmental concerns – sort of a merger between environmental concerns and traditional art.

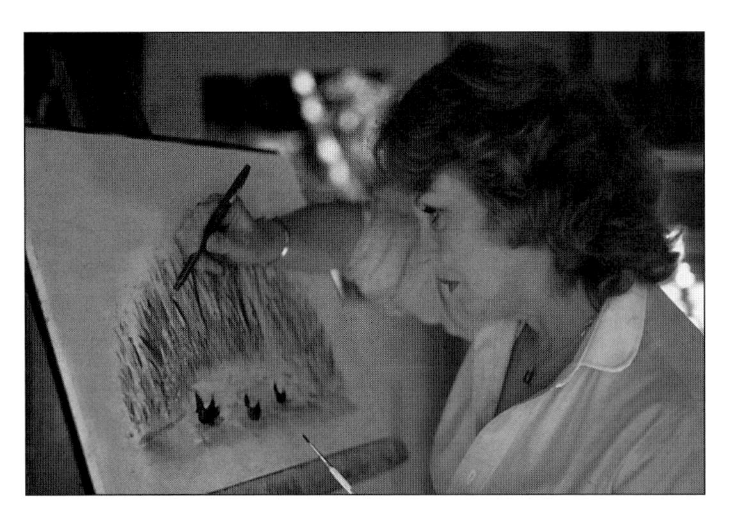

Above: Hazel the Artist

"Black Shadows" in black Belgium marble is a piece I donated to the Screen Actors Guild. It is polished black marble with white patches. It looks like shadows flying through the air.

A special piece is displayed in the Joe Paterno Library of Penn State University in Pennsylvania. When they asked me to contribute a piece for the library, it was weeks before I was able to envision the appropriate kind of sculpture. Then one night very late I thought, "Well, knowledge is books, books are knowledge, and knowledge is eternal." So I carved a big book, and then a smaller one on top of that, an even smaller one on top of that and, at the very top, an eternal flame. The sculpture, entitled "Knowledge is Eternal," stands in the entrance hall.

My daughter, Sally, once wrote of my work, "With a strong and sensitive touch, Miss Court's sculpture emerges in long, flowing, lyrical lines that form flight, shells, flowers, leaves, and oceanic shapes, often transforming her stone into a translucent piece, allowing light to flow through the material as though it is somewhat transparent. While Miss Court's technique focuses as well on organic and often sensuous forms, it is this play of light through her stone which heightens the contrast between mass and fantasy and gives her work its unique balance of opposites."

My deep gratitude goes to Diana Basehart and to Bernice Schachter who was honoured by the town of Pietrasanta for her contribution to its culture. I doubt I would have sculpted in marble, and had the opportunity to work in Italy where Michelangelo worked, if my dear friend Bernice Schachter – an

American – had not accepted me into her workshop. I am so grateful to the delightful Silverio for opening up his studio and his heart to us year after year. I recently learned, with great sadness, of his departure from us all. It was an era in my life never to be forgotten.

My gratitude goes also to Ivano Stampeggi who looked after us and really cared about our well-being. Every morning at eight o'clock, we got a lecture from him on politics, Italian-style. It was hilarious. Ivano departed this world, but not before he left a marvellous impression on all who stayed at the Hotel Italia.

I am so lucky to have walked the old streets, breathed the aromatic cooking, sipped the aged wine, and enjoyed the town of Pietrasanta – which means "holy stone." I toast the town!

THE DAME WHO CAME TO DINNER

Don was casting a TV special and could not find the right actress for the leading role. I asked him who he imagined in the part, if given a free choice. His reply surprised me.

"The English actress Dame Edith Evans. She is marvellous, marvellous. I should be so lucky."

To those who are very young and may not know who Dame Edith is, she was born in 1888, counts among her distinguished credits the films *The Whisperers*, *Tom Jones*, *The Madwoman of Chaillot* and *Look Back in Anger*, and the stage plays *The Chalk Garden* and *Waters of the Moon* with Dame Sybil Thorndike. She was always impressive in whatever role she played and never seemed to miss – like Maggie Smith and Judi Dench. She received Oscar nominations for *Tom Jones* and *The Chalk Garden*, and won a Golden Globe and Film Critics Circle Award for her performance as the frightened old lady in Bryan Forbes' *The Whisperers* (1967), for which she also received her third Oscar nomination.

"Why don't you ask her?" I said. "She can only say 'yes' or 'no.'"

"You're right," he said, with that wonderful twinkle in his eye. So she was approached, and to our amazement, she said she would be delighted.

"I have never worked in Hollywood before," said Dame Edith. "That would be a new adventure, dear boy. What fun!"

Dame Edith came like a ship in full sail – stately, and full of confidence and great charm. She flirted outrageously with Don, and I'm sure he returned the compliment. They had fun, and everybody enjoyed the show. Before she left, we thought we should throw a party for her. Don had heard that Basil Rathbone was in town. Many years previously, he and Dame Edith had played in *Romeo and Juliet* on Broadway, a production that became a legend in its time.

We invited about sixty people including Basil Rathbone, who was excited about seeing Dame Edith after so many years. Everything was in full swing, with many friends catching up with each other. Dame Edith stood in the hallway, welcoming everybody. Suddenly Rathbone appeared, flung his arms in the air, and screamed, "Darling! Darling!" She did the same, and a great scene took place, full of joy and laughter. When the scene was winding down, she rushed over to Don.

"Who was that I was talking to?" she asked.

"Why, that was Basil Rathbone," Don replied, surprised. "Remember? You played the nurse in *Romeo and Juliet* on Broadway with him."

Her hands flew up in the air, and she returned to him to play the whole scene again, with more gusto than ever. We laughed and tried to hear what was being said. All we heard was, "Darling, remember when…?" The rest was lost in nostalgic memories.

I had introduced Dame Edith to my mother. They seemed to enjoy each other's company, discovering they lived just a few miles apart in the country at Kent, England. Both loved gardening, and had won prizes for their roses.

"I want to sit next to your mother at dinner," she bellowed at me across the room.

"Of course you can," I said.

It was a memorable moment, watching my mother sitting next to Dame Edith, a very famous lady, talking about manure and compost and how big their roses bloomed, completely happy. The party was a wonderful success. I didn't want it to end. I wanted to just freeze-frame and keep it forever.

DAMIEN: OMEN II

In 1978, my husband was asked to direct the second *Omen* film. The first, produced by Harvey Bernhard, directed by Richard Donner and starring Gregory Peck, had been a tremendous success. The first and second *Omen* films dealt with good and evil. They showed us that the devil is everywhere – in business, politics and the minds of little children. One has only to think of Enron to be convinced of evil's infiltration into the world of big business.

It was one hell of a scary movie. Many things went wrong during the shooting, like a storm that nearly brought down the plane they were flying in.

Harvey said he really thought his life was about to end. Suddenly, it all cleared. The devil had done his work.

I did not have a part in the film, but I did accompany Don on location. I will never forget the night I arrived in Chicago, our first location for shooting. It was my first trip to that fascinating city. Snow was falling very gently, and lights twinkled on all the trees. As I arrived at the hotel, a black baseball player dressed in white mink from head to toe was waiting for a taxi. No woman could have looked better. It was one beautiful scene.

Harvey Bernhard was wonderful to work with – a laugh a minute. We became great friends with him and his charming wife, Lillian. Twenty years later, we still remain close friends.

William Holden was the star of *Omen II* and Lee Grant the female lead. Don had acted alongside Holden in *Stalag 17*, a war film that became a tremendous hit, and both men were excited to be working together again. William Holden was a charming man. He was never any trouble and showed infinite patience with other actors. There was a sadness about him I could never quite figure out – until Thanksgiving, when we had a special dinner for the cast and crew. Halfway through dinner, Holden turned to Don and said, "Got to go to my room, old boy."

I was concerned for Holden, but Don said, "Don't worry. He's okay, but he finds it hard to socialise at these sorts of functions since he gave up drinking." This was the answer to the mystery of the sadness I had felt from him. He had also split up with his long-time love, Stephanie Powers.

Chicago was a great location, and many outstanding horror moments took place in the Chicago railroads. The devil loved to push trains off their tracks.

The next stop was Wisconsin where a memorable scene was shot on the frozen Eagle River. In the scene, the actor Lew Ayres walks onto the ice and as he reaches the centre of the river, the ice cracks like a starburst, pulling him under and into the river. His body is visible through the ice for a good quarter mile. The cameraman freezes the frame on his body, and the end looks like a Bruegel painting. It's very impressive. See the film.

The Wisconsin cold was paralysing. With moon boots on our feet and special waterproof jackets made for us in a sky blue tie-dye design, we all looked like blue jays. There was lots of laughter all around.

Lillian Bernhard had spoken to one of the drivers and he had told her of a place where we could get some *very* interesting things. She asked me if I wanted to go buy some antiques, so we set off with another lady. We drove forever, and then changed cars and drivers. I was sure we were going to be kidnapped. Suddenly, after travelling for about a mile, in the middle of a forest a driveway appeared, and there was a large house.

Large glass doors swung open and, clutching Lillian's arm, I staggered up the steps with her, and into what looked to be a Vincent Price-style castle. Ahead of us were tables of impressive looking antiques, china, and glass. It all looked like the real stuff.

Coming towards us, a very large lady said, "Please look around and enjoy yourselves. See the "N" on this table? That stands for Napoleon."

There was the "N" alright. It looked like the real thing.

The lady moved on to another table. "This is Depression glass," she sang. "I'm sure American ladies know about that."

This English lady did not know about it, but I could guess – glass made in the Depression era. It was fascinating. Some was heavy and thick, other pieces were delicate and pink in colour. I bought a platter, six bowls, and six little plates, very delicate and finely etched. I still have them to this day. Maybe they are valuable. Lillian and her friend bought beautiful 18th century cups, saucers and plates. There were some incredible pieces, but we were jittery and anxious to get out of there. Out there in the middle of the forest, we had to wonder, where had all of these authentic pieces come from?

We said our goodbyes, and the first driver was waiting for us outside. We were so pleased to see him. He drove us back to the film set, and the crew laughed when we told them our story – laughed like they knew something we didn't. Our final verdict? Real, but stolen.

LOCATION: THE HOLY LAND

Our next location was Israel and, as I had never been there, there was great excitement. Sadly, William Holden was not coming, since he had no scenes in that part of the film. He did say that we would witness a magnificent sight if we stayed on the West Bank. At 5.00 a.m. the sun would rise and turn Jerusalem to pink.

We did stay on the West Bank, and we did see the sunrise. It was very mystical, a glorious sight. As the pink began to fade, time seemed to go backwards through the centuries and return to the present.

We travelled to Haifa, the Dead Sea, the city of Acre in the Western Galilee district in Northern Israel, and many other wonderful places.

UNESCO recently inscribed the old city of Acre on its coveted list of World Heritage sites. On a par with Constantinople and Alexandria, Acre is among the world's oldest continuously inhabited cities.

In Acre, I was fascinated to stand on the quayside where Richard the Lionheart and the crusaders had landed. Watching the water lapping the stones they had set foot upon, time stood still.

The marketplace was old, so old, a thousand years old. It was fascinating. I have never seen tomatoes so big they were more like melons. We were not allowed to photograph the women. When we tried, they put up their hands and said, "No, no, our souls will be lost forever."

In Acre, there was a stunning underground crusader's palace. For centuries, the winds of time had buried it with sand and earth. Then the 20th century excavated it when the British were occupying Israel. They built a prison over the palace site and Israeli soldiers were imprisoned there. They tunnelled their way to freedom and, in doing so, hit the palace. Twentieth Century Fox made it look beautiful. Doorways, pillars and arches were all preserved, and it looked like nothing had changed. *Omen II* showed it off to perfection. It is reached by a small elevator which seems so out of place with the crusader's palace.

I knew the ancient Phoenician city of Tyre was up the coast, about twenty-three miles north of Acre, jutting out of the Mediterranean Sea. In my teenage years, I had won first prize in my hometown of Sutton Coldfield for reciting poetry at a big Welsh competitive festival called an Eisteddfod. The winning poem I recited was "The Old Ships" by James Elroy Flecker. The opening verse begins, *"I have seen old ships, sail like swans asleep, beyond the village which, men still call Tyre…"* I was determined to "look towards Tyre" and asked Don's driver if he could take me to the coast.

Barbed wire bundles rolled for miles separating Israel and Lebanon. A little hut stood almost in the ocean. Looking up the coast, I remembered, *"…beyond the village which, men still call Tyre…"* Suddenly, I was thrown to the ground with the driver on top of me. Bullets were spraying all around. The Lebanese were having a go at Israel. Within seconds, Israeli planes were chasing them away. It was the first and last time I was shot at, and it was a terrifying experience.

My daughter, Sally, had been dating a very handsome man from Israel. He was a Druze. The Druze speak both Arabic and Hebrew, and are an offshoot of Islam but consider themselves a distinct religious community –

neither Muslim nor Jewish. He had talked about Mount Carmel, his tremendous Israeli village overlooking the Mediterranean Sea. He would always say to me, "If you ever go to Israel, you must visit a Druze village."

The next day, I asked Lillian and her friend if they would enjoy visiting a Druze village. Don's personal driver said he knew of a perfect village that we would find fascinating, and said he would love to take us. We drove up a beautiful mountain. High on the mountaintop, nesting in wispy white clouds was a village all white and clean. It took our breath away.

We stopped outside the village and walked up the dirt road in silence, treading on history. The houses were snow white and well kept. All roads were just dirt, but swept clean. There was a small pottery gallery, and we ventured in. The owner spoke English and welcomed us. Lovely plates hung on the walls. When we asked who the artist was, the owner said, "My brother. He lives in New York part of the year, and sells many plates." I wanted to buy one, and so did Lillian. They were all so inventive it was hard to make up our minds. Finally, we made our choices and paid a large sum for our plates. Apparently his brother was well known. Today mine hangs on the wall of my mountain home in Lake Tahoe, California.

Carrying our plates, we wandered up the brown dirt street. Suddenly, I smelled new bread. Following my nose along the white walls, I stopped at large doors, opened a little. I had found the bread spot. Suddenly, the doors were opened wide, and a beautiful woman swathed in red silk beckoned for us to enter. She laughed as I sniffed the wonderful smell of bread. We were welcomed into a magnificent patio with exquisite cushions placed on stone benches. One wall was covered in gorgeous coffee cups – Wedgwood and Crown Derby from England, Dresden from France, and so on, round the world. I managed to convey to her how impressive the wall was to me. She was so pleased, and let us know the coffee was coming, indicating for us to sit on the cushions.

We did not speak each other's language, but it didn't matter. Both Lillian and her friend said they could not drink the coffee because of their stomachs. I gave them big elbow jabs and said, "We'll drink every drop." Coffee came and it was very thick. I had visions of stomach aches on the way home. The coffee cups were Limoges, and so beautiful. Through signs and finger pointing we conveyed to this lovely lady how much we appreciated everything. Her husband, the baker, came and shook our hands. We drank our coffee, thanked them many times, and said our goodbyes. They hugged us and gave us each a little hand-woven scarf. I didn't know if they were Druze or what, but it didn't matter. Though I will never see them again, I will never forget them. It was a very special moment in my life.

MORE COFFEE

Two days after my experience in the Druze village, Don had a day to relax and be with me. Someone suggested we go visit Jericho. Located in the West Bank, Palestine, many believe it to be the oldest continuously occupied settlement in the world. My ears pricked up and of course, I thought of the *"and the walls came tumbling down"* story from the Bible about Jericho. "Wonderful!" I yelled, so my husband got a driver who spoke English, and away we went.

My memory of Jericho is a rambling old town, large palm trees, and a lot of very colourful Arabs. Today I'm sure it's probably changed drastically, and is probably modernised. We wandered slowly round old buildings and suddenly into a little square where a group of Arabs were chatting and laughing round a little brazier [a coal heater].

One very, very colourful Arab was wearing over his white robe a flowing turquoise coat. The colour is still with me today. He was a powerful character, very handsome, his face burnt to a wonderful bronze from decades of sun. When he saw us, he raised his arms high in the air and shouted, "Ah, Americans. Welcome to coffee." Once again, we were served coffee in gorgeous cups. The coffee was as good as the aroma. Then he linked arms with both of us, and we danced round the little brazier. He was singing, and his friends joined in.

Reluctant to go, we hugged each other and said goodbye. It was a moment neither Don nor I ever forgot. Once again, coffee had united three different nations. With the world in great turmoil, one wonders sometimes if maybe coffee isn't the answer. The way of simplicity can be powerful.

OMEN III: THE FINAL CONFLICT

In 1981, Harvey Bernhard, producer of *the Omen* films, decided to make *Omen III: The Final Conflict*, the third in the trilogy. Don, my husband, could not direct this one. It had to be an English director – rules and all that. Graham Baker was chosen as the director, and he was very good. I never heard him shout. He was really a very nice person. Sam Neill played the devil, and it was all very spooky.

Above: Hazel and artist Fred Yates in Pietrasanta, Italy

The film was to be shot in Cornwall, England, and in the North at Yorkshire, at the thousand years old Fountains Abbey. As I have said, Cornwall has always fascinated me. There is something about stones sitting in a field for four thousand years that really gets to me.

Harvey's wife, Lillian, had never been to that part of England and was anxious to see it, so Harvey asked me to accompany them and show Lillian all the things I loved about Cornwall. It was not intended that I should have a part in the film. I was simply going along for the journey to Cornwall – but, as you'll soon discover, Fate had her own ideas.

First shooting was at Roche Rock, near the china clay pits and not far from St. Austell. Roche Rock is a medieval tower of crumbling rocks set in the middle of a moor. God only knows what is going on in the earth around there. Legend has it that, for the love of Isolde, Tristan of the famous opera *Tristan and Isolde*, threw himself to his death from this rock. Considering the setting – in Cornwall among four thousand year old stones – I wouldn't be at all surprised if the legend were true.

There was a hunt scene set in the village near Roche Rock. Horses, hounds and the cast were ready to go, but where was the lady who was to hand the stirrup cup of wine to the huntsman? She was nowhere to be found.

"Hazel," yelled Harvey, "get in there with the jugs of wine!"

Believing that no one would recognise me playing a part I wasn't cast in, I rushed right in and did what I was told, thinking nothing of it. I was wrong,

wrong, wrong to think no one would realise it was me. Fan mail poured in, and it seemed the whole world had seen me in that scene.

Unhappy with the food at the hotel where we were staying, Harvey went hunting and found Boscundle Manor, a small 15th Century hotel. The manor was run by Mary and Andrew Flint, a wonderful couple, and the food was highly recommended. Mary, a great chef, cooked all the food for the guests except breakfast. Andrew cooked heavenly breakfasts which I can still taste and smell to this day – eggs, bacon, fresh mushrooms, tomatoes.

Sam Neill, Harvey, his wife Lillian, Graham Baker and I all went to dinner in a bunch. While we were drinking in the bar, suddenly Sam Neill said, "Who painted those pictures? They are magnificent! Charming!"

"Oh, that's our Fred," said Mary Flint. "He lives locally."

We all chorused, "Can we buy?"

"Oh, yes, yes, just a minute," said Mary, "I'll ring up Fred and see if he's home." Off she trotted to the kitchen. We could hear her beautiful pitched English accent, saying, "Fred, the Americans are here. They want to buy."

Hours later, still no Fred.

"We have to go," Harvey said. "I've got to get up early in the morning."

At that moment, someone started banging on the baronial front door. It was Fred, who had arrived with armfuls of paintings. Through the door, I could see his little Mini Minor car. It was covered in oil paint, and it looked like he used it as his easel.

"I had car trouble," Fred breathlessly explained, and in he stumbled.

His paintings were whimsical, charming, and very, very good. Well, we all bought a painting, and some of us two. I think that was the beginning of great things for Fred Yates. Born and bred in Manchester, Northern England, Yates went on to become very famous, and he also became a close friend of mine, as did Mary and Andrew. Fred's work can be seen on Albemarle Street in London at the John Martin Gallery.

It was a night to remember. Indeed, any day or night with Fred is a time to remember. He is one of a kind in this world, a real character.

Above Top: Hazel & Lillian Bernhard. A cameo in Omen III is Hazel's last screen appearance

Above Bottom: Artist Fred Yates

Our next location stop was Fountains Abbey in Yorkshire where the devil was killed, but I didn't go. Except for my accidental role in the movie, I wasn't actually playing a part in the film, so I returned to America where I was needed in a film I was doing. Years later, my publisher, Bruce Sachs and his wife took me there. It is over a thousand years old, and really tremendous. It speaks history through every archway, and is really an incredible place. If you ever have a chance to visit, you will not be disappointed.

Omen III: The Final Conflict was successful, like all the other *Omen* films. Perhaps someday there will be a fourth.

ABOUT THE WORD "GONE"

The year was 1998, in November. We were still living at San Vicente. Don was troubled with his right foot and had difficulty walking. The doctor said blood thinners were necessary, but time went on and there were no improvements. One day, I could see that the pain was almost too much for him. I had been expecting this but when reality stares you in the face, it's a different matter.

My son Jonathan looked at me and said, "It's the hospital for Dad." Jonathan and his friend Billy carried Don down the stairs on a chair.

We reached UCLA Hospital still intact with Don making jokes, very gently. We made contact with Don's doctors and they made him comfortable. I left the hospital feeling that my husband was okay. He was still making jokes and flirting with the nurses and that seemed reassuring. He did not look ill. I will never get over what happened – he was still my handsome man.

Don's daughters Avery and Anne had been in France at the time, celebrating Avery's birthday. His ex-wife Phyllis – we were one big extended family – had been with them. They returned a few days after Don was admitted to the hospital.

Nothing had changed. Blood thinners did not seem to be making any difference. We were all warned that amputation was a possibility. I kept saying to myself, "I did not hear those words," but again, I came face to face with reality. Two weeks later, Don lost his right foot. It is hard to write about – those were not the best of times, but we carried on. One must.

He recovered, but he still required a great deal of treatment. We were all with him each day, and everything seemed to be fine. Then, towards Christmas, I heard the doctors talking about the other foot. The same problem was happening all over again.

Left: Don Taylor (1920 – 1998). This is Hazel's favourite photo of her beloved Don.

On the 28th of December, 1998, the hospital called and told me to get there right away. They told me that he probably only had a few hours left of his life. I will never know how I got to the hospital.

His doctor told me that one thing after another was breaking down. The domino effect was starting. At 11.00 that morning, with all the family around him, Don left us. Gone.

Gone – a terrible word. My lovely husband, a very special man and lover, and my best friend in the entire world had left me. Gone – one of the most powerful words in the English language.

Now, several years later, I still love him. I still talk to him. There will never be another Don for me. I have changed my mind a little about the word "gone." Someone you love deeply is gone at the moment of death, yes. But very slowly, they drift back to you. It's true, it's a drifting. Then they stay with you ever afterwards.

A DAY IN MAY OF 1999

The San Vicente house had been sold. It was my last day in the house. Packing my car up to the roof, I was ready for the long drive that lay ahead of me. I was off to Northern California, Lake Tahoe and the High Sierra mountains. Years before, Don had bought me a little mountain lodge because I loved nature and all it tells us. It was our very special place, a romantic getaway. I was hoping that there I would be able to sort myself out a little.

My son Jonathan had a beautiful Staffordshire terrier named Coco. I called her, but she was nowhere to be found. Finally, I discovered her at the bottom of the garden, curled up behind a bush. She was near my painting studio, where we had spent many hours together, creating. She knew that something was happening, that life was changing for her. Her lovely, sleek, silky body was trembling, and her wonderful soulful eyes questioned me. I stroked her, telling her all would be well, that Jono would soon join us, and that Sally was already waiting in Tahoe. Coming into my arms for a cuddle, she calmed down and we walked to the car, where she would sit behind the driver's seat – her spot for travelling.

Phyllis had come by to see if I was okay. I thought this very kind of her. We hugged and both shed a tear as we looked up at the house – so powerful – where we had both lived and loved the same man, both actresses, appreciating and respecting each other, which through the years had made life easy and enjoyable.

NOTHING STAYS THE SAME

I circled the San Vicente driveway for the last time, saying goodbye to the house, to the giant cedar tree I had loved, and to the beautiful front lawn where so many marvellous parties and weddings had been enjoyed. Driving down the lovely driveway, my heart was breaking. Thirty years I had lived there. My thoughts turned to all the widows who had been in the same situation. My heart broke for them, too. I was not unique.

A new life had begun. No more film pressures or disappointments. Hollywood had been good to me, but it was over. A wonderful husband, a beautiful home and special friends were now never-to-be-forgotten memories. I knew it was over.

Above: The view from Hazel's Bear Creek cabin

As I drove down John Scott Trail seven thousand feet up in the High Sierra Mountains in Lake Tahoe, I began to drive slowly. I was approaching my new life in a little "Hansel & Gretel" cottage in Bear Creek. Suddenly high on a rock to my right, looking down at me, was a magnificent wolf-like creature. To this day, I cannot be sure what he was – wolf, coyote, hybrid? He looked to be more wolf than anything. I stopped the car, rolled down the window, and told him he was very beautiful. As I looked into those amber coloured eyes, it was as if I saw the whole world from beginning to end. We locked eyes for a moment, and then he tossed his head and was gone. Tears rolled down my face. It was an experience never to leave me.

Next day he came and sunbathed on my deck. Every night at six o'clock, he was on the pathway, looking at the house. I began to think he enjoyed the evening news. Every night, I put a piece of bread outside – only one. Then at the end of winter, he came at the usual time, but there was a difference. He stood under the strong light on the pathway, like a good actor hitting his mark perfectly, and choosing the best, most powerful light to illuminate him. For a good two or three minutes he stopped at the house, then he turned slowly and left. I knew he would never return. Wolfie was moving on – just like his friend from Los Angeles. We were both on our way.

RETURNING HOME TO BIRMINGHAM

In the year 2004, I was asked to attend a film convention at the big convention centre in Birmingham. I had not returned to my roots in nearly sixty years.

Barry Poland, a private detective, and his wife said they would drive me there and take me to Wylde Green where I grew up. These two lovely friends gave me so much of their time, and I was well looked after. As we were driving from Birmingham to Wylde Green, I noticed that things had changed, but not too drastically. I remembered so much.

Above: Chocolate the Bear outside Hazel's home in Bear Creek

Next thing I knew, we were at Wylde Green Post Office and I yelled, "Turn left, down Vesey Road." The road ran into Eastern Road like a T-crossing. There, suddenly, was my old home, exactly as I had left it, with the streetlight outside the front door. I could hear my Grandma, sighing, "The magic has gone. No more lamplighters."

The area had wonderful Victorian and Georgian houses and I was thrilled to see they were all still there and in excellent condition. On Eastern Road, I saw the house where the Levik Studio had been, where I had my first picture taken with my sister when I was age one year.

So many memories rushed to be remembered – growing up, the war, bombings, friends that I had lost. How different the world was then, in spite of the war. I walked two miles to school and two miles back. We never had a car. Drugs were unheard of, and sex was still a romantic affair. The next door neighbours were a part of our family, from caring about them to popping in to see them each day. In spite of the war, my family was happy, squeezing the most and best out of the days.

I had to see if my chestnut tree and the air raid shelter were there at the bottom of my garden, so we all trotted down to the railway station. A lovely lady came out and asked if she could help us. She was the station mistress – not master. Yes, things had changed a little. I told her of my desire to see the air raid shelter at the bottom of my old garden. She was delighted to help us, locked up the booking office, and escorted us down the platform.

As we walked along the platform to the spot where I remembered my chestnut tree to be, little shivers went up and down my spine. Time fell away, and I was a little girl again, climbing the tree and weaving my dreams. Starting to run, I saw the chestnut tree ahead, leaning over the railing, looking older and thinner. Mission completed, the air raid shelter was now residing peacefully in the past, wearing its coat of many vines.

There were two more places I had to see – my old school, Boldmere, and St. Michael's, the church where every Sunday I enjoyed participating in the service with Mother, Father, and Grandma Blockley. My memory serves me well. There was great dignity and stability in my upbringing. The war gave me strength to live life well and enjoy each day. This I think I have done.

As I got back in the car, I said goodbye to my roots and to my early beginnings. I loved my parents all over again, and thanked them for how well they brought me up, and for all the good memories. Dear wonderful, special Mum and Dad.

Returning to the United States after a successful trip to Birmingham, many nostalgic thoughts kept running through my mind. How did I get from Birmingham, England to the High Sierras, seven thousand feet high? As a child in school, I had looked at pictures of the High Sierras in my geography books, but I never dreamed I would live on top of them.

I love these mountains. The people here are true mountain people. They may not invite you to dinner, but they do look after you, popping by with a snow blower to clear the walk outside my cabin after a storm. When the first few flakes of snow appear, I look out of my window. The first snowfall of the winter is always the best and most beautiful. Invariably it is gentle snow. If you listen carefully, you can hear the quiet voice of the snow saying, "Hello, I'm back."

Looking back, I have enjoyed my life. There has been many a bump in the road, but we all have them. We learn from the bumps and carry on. The road of my life has led me here, to these incredible views, to this place where I look to the big granite mountains. So many things got me to the top of the High Sierras – all the movies and TV shows I made in America, and marrying Don who bought me this chalet.

One day recently, I was talking to my son Jonathan on the deck of my house and suddenly I noticed there was a bear eating a cinnamon bun I had put out for the birds on a three hundred-year-old tree stump that the birds use as a table. He was a two-year-old gorgeous bear I had seen before. When the bear saw Jonathan on the deck, he turned and went off down the lane.

In a loud voice, Jonathan called after him, "Chocolate! Chocolate! You don't have to go. Come back and finish your cinnamon bun." The bear turned around, looked at us, and came back. It was remarkable. This is why I call Jonathan "Dr. Dolittle" – he speaks to animals and they understand him.

These mountains give me strength and transport me into another world. Sometimes when I am sitting on the deck, I can hear voices in the sky – the voices that never die. I listen, and something comes across me, guiding me. Those who have lived, in a sense, live forever – in those quiet voices whispering forever around the world. As I get older, I get the guidance I need almost before I have even formed the thought or asked the question.

I have turned this place into a museum. Everywhere I have travelled, I have brought something back with me and, as I look around my house, I am reminded – Italian plates, jugs from France. These are the things I want around me, the things I want to look at every day. To hell with cream carpets and off-white walls!

My life in the city is gone – no more Los Angeles for me. No more London. Just as I did when I was a little girl, I still hug trees. I love nature and gather my strength from her. As I sit on my deck, the world beyond is talking to me, guiding my path. In the summer, it is particularly wonderful and, of course, I am on good terms with every chipmunk and squirrel. The bluebirds around here are enormous and they have learned that 7.00 is feeding time.

If I am a minute late, they let me hear about it. "I'm coming," I cry, and set their food out on the tree stump. Sometimes I think, if the chipmunks and the bluebirds can learn to live together, surely we, who have voices to speak…

America has been very kind to me. I once asked Andre Driollet, a French restaurateur who opened "The Bicycle Shop Café" on Wilshire Boulevard in Los Angeles, why he was in Los Angeles and not France. His answer has always remained with me. "If you want something," he said, "America is where you can make it happen."

There is so much to see here in America. Each state is different and has its own personality. It is a magnificent country. Zion National Park, Bryce Canyon and the Grand Canyon all brought tears to my eyes the first time I saw them. Nature is so beautiful and so powerful, and I hope it will be preserved and cared for.

As much as I love America, and as much as I have learned from America, I am English, bred and born. Nothing can change that fact. The English seeds were growing long before the American ones, and I will never be anything but English – and very proud of it.

THE CIRCLES OF LIFE

I believe in the circles of life. One starts at the top of the circle and travels around, and then one day, you are back at the top again. I have always felt this way about life. Even when I was a teenager, I noticed that things seemed to be happening in a circle. The beginning and ending of marriages and lives – the end of my life with Dermot, the end of my life with Don, and then the end of their lives – these are circles, too. Several years after Don's devastating death in 1998, Dermot's death in early 2005 came as a terrible shock to Sally and to me.

In writing this book, I started at the beginning with the story of my Grandma Blockley leaving England for the first time to travel to France to see her daughter, Annie, who was very ill.

While finishing my book, a letter arrived from a Mary Thompson in Wellington, Shropshire, England. To my surprise, she had found me through an interview I did at Penn State University, and had asked them to forward a letter to me. Her maiden name was Mary Blockley. Life had come full circle. She is a third cousin once removed. She told me that she had collected every piece of memorabilia that she could find related to me. We have become friends, and she has researched my family tree. Yes, I am half Welsh. My romantic grandma's name was Mary Jones, and she was from Montgomeryshire in Wales. She married a David Blockley and gave birth to my mother who was christened Mary Magdalene because she was born on Easter Sunday morning.

She also researched aunts and uncles, which was fascinating for me. Somewhere I have a Blockley who owns a sheep farm, going back to the 1500s. It is quite famous in the Welsh mountains. I can't wait to go and meet these relatives I have never seen.

I remember I always used to hear my mother speak about Great Aunt Caroline who had her own "carriage and pair." I said to Mary, "I wonder where Aunt Caroline fits in," and we both thought perhaps she had been made up. Then I found her, and just like Grandma Blockley and her beloved David, Aunt Caroline had married well, and her husband died young. Life had once again come full circle.

Now I am halfway to Heaven and my life has come full circle. It is a good circle.

Art has been a big part of the circle for me. I love Van Gogh and his Starry Night. It leaps off the canvas and suddenly you are there in the middle of that nocturnal scene. I adore Rembrandt.

I have a couple of paintings by a Ukranian artist. One is a painting of a granny and grandpa, who live in the mountains where the apples grow. In the picture, they are sitting together on a bench with apples all around them. As I sit here on my mountain and gaze out at the snow, I look at his paintings – one of a man trudging at night through the snow on the way to his village, another on his sleigh returning from his village.

It reminds me of a fable. Somebody said to a Ukranian painter one day, "Come with me, I can make you famous and rich!"

"Famous? Rich?" he said. "Why do I want these things?"

"Well, then you could have everything you want!"

"But I have everything I want already," he replied. "I love my family, they are here with me, I can paint them. I have my village here, and I love my village. What more would I want?"

I hope you, my readers, have enjoyed my reminiscences about my life. The last little bit of the tapestry has yet to be lived. I have no idea what I will get up to, but it will be something enjoyable. I can't wait to come back again, and do it all over – maybe as an archaeologist next time. It warms my heart to know my work will remain, and be seen by people, long after I am gone.

Just in case I should pop off to Heaven in the night, I always remember to wash up, punch up the cushions and straighten up after a dinner party. I wouldn't want everyone to come in and find it a mess. It's very English of me. In fact, one time I awakened in the night to discover that my left leg was funny. I had a mini-stroke. Even though my leg was "off", I walked on it, thinking I've got to get myself to the hospital, but first I must tidy up a bit. So I cleaned the bathroom, the living room, made the bed. I cleaned the whole bloody house. By the time I had done all that, my leg was better. I sat and laughed at myself, thinking, "Well, there you go. That's my mother in me."

It is the same thing when I go into town. I always make sure I am put together. I make my face up, and dress properly, and people stop me in the street and say something nice, like "Oh, I love that sweater." Especially when I wear my emerald green cloak from Ireland, people always stop by and say "hello."

In watching *The Man Who Could Cheat Death* again the other day, I thought to myself, "I believe every age has its beauty." At every different age, I believe there are gifts to us and things we can do which we do not do when we are seventeen. There is a wonderful kind of experiment in growing old. You learn a lot and you keep on learning – if you are listening. Listening to what is going on inside and what is going on around you is very important, and these days a lot of people do not listen.

Yes, every age has its beauty, but in looking back, I did not understand how beautiful I was then. I was aware that I did have a certain beauty, but it is easier if you don't really know. I think it is better that way. As the song says, *"Those were the days my friend, I thought they'd never end."* I never did think those days would end, and yet, here we are, and life has come full circle.

OTHER GREAT TITLES FROM TOMAHAWK

"One of the best independent publishing houses of niche market title books in the world" – Cinema Retro

Hammer Films - The Elstree Studios Years

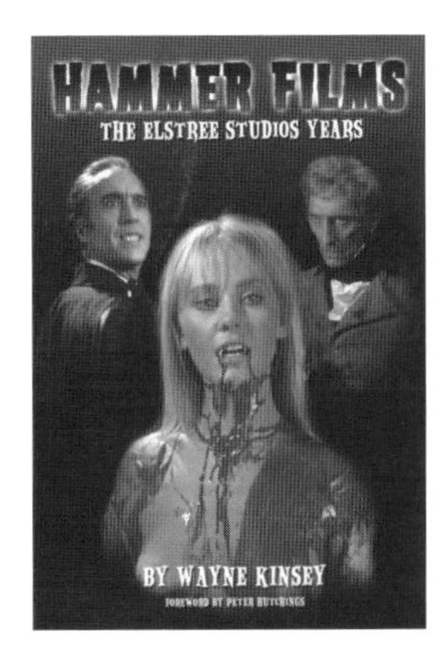

by Wayne Kinsey
Foreword by Peter Hutchings, Northumbria University
Lavishly illustrated with over 700 rare B/W images

ISBN 10: 0-9531926-2-8   ISBN 13: 978-0-9531926-2-5

Wayne Kinsey reveals the story of Hammer Films from 1967 to the present day, following the highs and lows of the company as it bedded into its new home at Elstree. Based on extensive oral history recording with Hammer personnel, the book describes in fascinating detail how the studio would plummet from one of the most successful British film companies and proud recipients of the Queen's Award for Industry, to the depths of bankruptcy within a single decade. As the British Censor relaxed, Hammer took full advantage, steeping their films in the seventies with sex and nudity as well as ever increasing gore. Even better than Kinsey's previous volume, the acclaimed *Hammer Films – The Bray Studios Years*, this book is heavily illustrated throughout by rare, never before published photos and documents, many taken behind the scenes of the famous "House that Dripped Blood".

"This is the story of Hammer's failure; of its failure to update successfully its horror formula, to engage with new markets, to regenerate itself. Kinsey shows that this was not for want of trying, and indeed a sense of Hammer's desperation becomes apparent at certain moments. Particularly revealing in this respect are Hammer's encounters with the British film censors - which are recorded here in some detail. Take this book not as a memorial, but instead as a record of an enduring fascination with one of the most extraordinary enterprises in British cinema history."
Peter Hutchings (from his foreword)

So You Wanna Be A Director

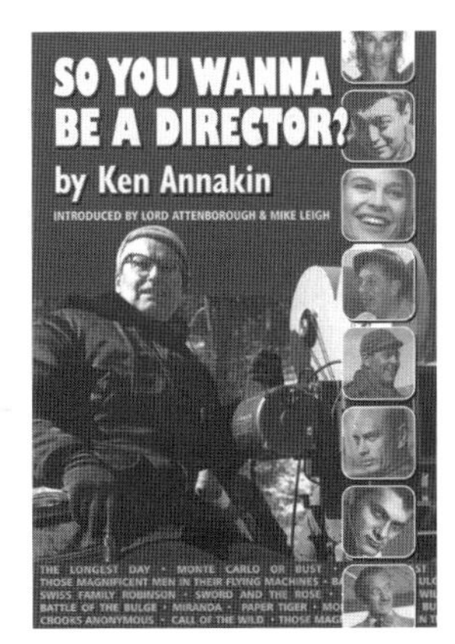

by Ken Annakin

ISBN: 0-953 1926-5-2

Anakin Skywalker? The name is George Lucas's tribute to one of his favourite directors, Yorkshire-born Ken Annakin – one of THE international film directors of the post-war era. This is his story in his own words, delivered with the style and humour that have made so many of his films famous the world over.

Ken Annakin was one of the greatest international film directors. The last of the English directors to make it on the international arena (others included Hitchcock and Lean), this 'no holds barred' autobiography traces Annakin's career from his early British films through to Hollywood. He has directed, written and produced over fifty feature films in Africa, India, Malaysia, Scandinavia, China, Europe and America. *So You Wanna Be A Director?* is an entertaining and witty travelogue, as well as an important document of film history.

Annakin's films include: Swiss Family Robinson, The Longest Day, Battle of the Bulge, Those Magnificent Men in Their Flying Machines, Miranda as well as three of Disney's greatest films.

The book provides personal and revealing insights into film personalities including:
Claudette Colbert, Jack Hawkins, David Niven, Rod Steiger, Henry Fonda, Robert Ryan, Julie Christie, Glynis Johns, Charles Bronson, Peter Ustinov, Dorothy McGuire, Edward G. Robinson, Raquel Welch, Tony Curtis, Olivia de Havilland, Vittorio de Sica, Charlton Heston, Robert Wagner, Peter Sellers, Terry Thomas, Darryl F. Zanuck, Walt Disney and many more.

Annakin's book is forthright and pulls no punches. It has become a classic among directors' autobiographies. Annakin details the dizzying heights and bleak lows of his career. This master of "family entertainment" sounds a loud clarion call for a return to motion pictures that are fun for all of the family.

TO VIEW OUR FULL CATALOGUE VISIT
www.tomahawkpress.com
Full secure online ordering

OTHER GREAT TITLES FROM TOMAHAWK

"One of the best independent publishing houses of niche market title books in the world" – *Cinema Retro*

Greasepaint and Gore – The Hammer Monsters of Roy Ashton

by Bruce Sachs and Russell Wall

ISBN: 0-953 1926-0-1

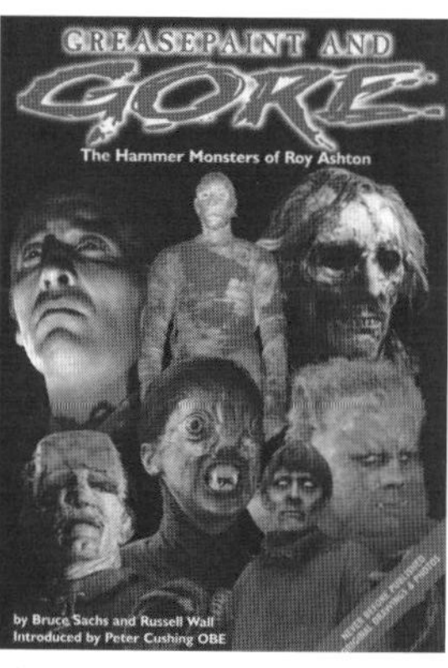

When you hear the words "Hammer Films", you instantly conjure up mental images of monsters and vampires. Behind the scenes was one man working flat out to produce those wonderful creatures. That man was Roy Ashton, and it was he who created all of the make-up effects for mummies, werewolves and Gothic horrors. Greasepaint and Gore takes a look into the props wardrobe and make up unit where Ashton, long before computer technology existed, created his own high standards of magical illusions. When Roy passed away in 1995, the authors began to collect his impressive series of preparatory sketches and have married these up with studio shots of the completed article as well as rare pictures of their subject busy at work. This is a remarkable collection and it is appropriate that there is a permanent home to the Roy Ashton Collection at the National Museum of Photography Film and Television. The Museum's acquisition of this important work was the first time ever that National Lottery money had been spent on film heritage.

With an introduction from the late Peter Cushing OBE, who had the opportunity to watch Roy Ashton at work countless times (after all make-up can also make you look glamorous as well as horrific), this is a demonstration of a true professional at work. Greasepaint and Gore catalogues the largest single collection of Hammer production artefacts in existence, and is a must have for any horror... or indeed any film fan!

Nevermore: The Edgar Allan Poe Films of Roger Corman

by David Del Valle and Sam Umland – Available 2009

ISBN 10: 0-9531926-9-5 ISBN 13: 978-0-9531926-9-4

Between 1960 and 1964, the legendary Roger Corman created eight motion pictures that have become known as the "Poe Cycle," elevating the careers of both himself and Vincent Price to cult status around the world. Nearly half a century later these films are staples in most DVD collections of anyone who admires the cinema of the Fantastic.

Nevermore: The Edgar Allan Poe Films of Roger Corman is the long-awaited book that details and analyses these highly important films. This book has been 30 years in the making! *Nevermore* will include:

Hundreds of rare images never seen before from each film

Commentaries from Vincent Price and Roger Corman.

Special observations by Barbara Steele, Elizabeth Shepherd, Joyce Jameson and Hazel Court as the leading ladies of the series.

Exclusive interviews with the actors and artisans that made the Poe films

Rare poster art from around the world

Extra material on the Poe films made after Corman with exclusive interviews with Gordon Hessler and Samuel Z Arkoff

Archivist and film historian David Del Valle in collaboration with Professor Sam Umland have fashioned a film by film analysis of Roger Corman's Poe films including the Poe-inspired films made after Corman left AIP to pursue other projects. The unique combination of Prof. Umland's insights into the literary landscape of Poe in concert with Mr. Del Valle's twenty five years of research interviewing all the participants in the Poe series now culminates in *Nevermore: The Edgar Allan Poe Films of Roger Corman*.

Nevermore: The Edgar Allan Poe Films of Roger Corman is the "dream within a dream" for aficionados of these films which have never left the imagination of the generation that grew up watching them.